THE GOLDEN BOOK
OF IMMORTALITY

THE
GOLDEN BOOK
OF
IMMORTALITY

A TREASURY OF TESTIMONY

Compiled and Edited by

T H O M A S   C U R T I S   C L A R K

and

H A Z E L   D A V I S   C L A R K

A S S O C I A T I O N   P R E S S
NEW YORK

To the Memory
of Our Parents
who have passed through death
into Life

ACKNOWLEDGMENTS

Acknowledgment is gratefully made of the generous co-operation of both contributors and publishers in the compilation of this anthology. The compilers have made every effort to trace the ownership of all copyrighted material. Should there be any question concerning the use of any selections, regret is expressed for unconscious error.

Sincere thanks are due the Christian Century Foundation for permission to reprint selections from *The Pulpit*. Grateful appreciation also is expressed to Harry Emerson Fosdick, Charles Clayton Morrison, William P. Merrill, M. H. Lichliter, Carl Knudsen, Ernest M. Howse, Alfred W. Swan, Charles W. Kegley, and Herbert B. Smith, who granted personal permission to quote freely from their contributions to that magazine. Acknowledgment is also made of the co-operation of the *Christian Century* in granting permission for the inclusion of selections from an article by Robert J. McCracken which appeared in that magazine; Dr. McCracken, too, is to be thanked for his personal permission.

Thanks are due Houghton Mifflin Company for permission to quote from the poetical works of Whittier, Emerson, and Aldrich; also the Macmillan Company for poems by Browning and Tennyson.

Arthur H. Compton granted permission to use an excerpt from an address, "Life After Death from the Point of View of a Scientist," which was delivered at the University of Chicago.

The poems by Edwin Markham are included by permission of his son, Virgil Markham.

THE COMPILERS

FOREWORD

A certain lawyer lost his devoted wife by a tragic death. He was heartbroken and in desperation he called his minister. As the two talked of the hope of immortality the bereaved husband was comforted. Yet, accustomed as he was to plain statements and sure evidence, he said to his pastor, with eager concern: "But why doesn't God write it across the sky—that there is a future life?"

Although the prevailing mood of people today is perhaps one of going along with the life that now is—"Earth is enough," "One world at a time"—there are probably more questions asked today concerning immortality than ever before in the world's history. The tragedy of war has snuffed out the lives of millions of promising young men. Bereft parents, brothers and sisters, are asking the question, "Why?" But they ask also the deeper-going question, "Whither?"

Among Christians there has always been the "solid certainty" as to the future life brought to his followers by Christ. However, it is a rather surprising fact that even in the churches there are today many who are troubled by a nebulous uncertainty concerning the Easter assertion that life persistently triumphs over death.

It is hoped that this book, with its intimations and hopes and confident assurances, may lend help to multitudes who would like to believe that "there is more to life than appears in the earthly scene, that its height and depth are greater and its reaches wider than can be stated in terms of the visible and tangible."

God has not written a sure promise of immortality "across the sky," but he has put the conviction of eternity in countless hearts. And some of these confident "hearts" bring inspiring testimony in these pages.

THOMAS CURTIS CLARK

CONTENTS

FEAR DEATH? THERE IS NO DEATH!

DAWN!

GREET THE UNSEEN WITH A CHEER!

ETERNITY—HERE AND NOW

Faith That Looks Through Death

EASTER HORIZONS

Heaven—the "Other Room"

We Believe in Immortality

TESTIMONY OF THE POETS

INTIMATIONS
OF IMMORTALITY

From Nature, Life, Literature

INTIMATIONS
OF IMMORTALITY

"Sight of That Immortal Sea"

Hence in a season of calm weather
   Though inland far we be,
Our Souls have sight of that immortal sea
   Which brought us hither,
   Can in a moment travel thither,
And see the Children sport upon the shore,
And hear the mighty waters rolling evermore.

WILLIAM WORDSWORTH

An Intimation of Immortality

It is right and proper that we should consider such intimations in nature and life that seem to support the idea of immortality. For instance, there is nothing more firmly established in science than the laws of conservation of matter and of force. No single atom in creation can go out of existence, according to the scientists; it only changes in form. We cannot burn up anything; we simply change it from a solid to a gaseous state. Neither is any energy or force ever destroyed; it is only changed from one form to another—steam into electricity, electricity into light or music or X-rays. If this principle holds good of matter and force, is it not likely to hold good of that form of force which we call life?

BURRIS JENKINS

Life Persistently Triumphs

Immortality is indicated in a fascinating way in your physical body. There life persistently triumphs over death in that process of constant death and resurrection which science calls metabolism. In your body, cells must die in order that new cells may be born and life may continue. Your physician will tell you that unless your body dies and changes cells at least every seven years, it runs the risk of perishing. Of persons over thirty years of age, who has a single particle with which he was born? Not one. Thus surely does life persistently change and triumph over death in your innermost experience. Here, then, is a compelling illustration of the Easter assertion: Life persistently triumphs over death.

CHARLES W. KEGLEY

God Is Life!

God is life. Life flows in upon me. Man receives life, but man does not give it. Life itself is the giver. It flows in at birth, it flows out at death; but it did not begin at the one, and it does not end at the other. It is eternal, it is all-pervasive. God is life, the life of all things. His life is manifested in myriads of forms, manifested everywhere. There is not a clod of mud that does not manifest the life of God. There is not a flower, a bird upon the wing, a cloud drifting in the sky, no lowly creature of the water or of the forest that does not manifest the life of God under one of its innumerable phases. God is life! . . . Life eternal is not merely life long drawn out; it is life made full.

FREDERICK W. NORWOOD

Belief in Endless Life Universal

The fact that the idea of unending life is so universal in all times and among all peoples would indicate that there is some foundation for it. Ideas are the most real things in the world; they do not spring up spontaneously and without reality behind them. There is always a ground for an idea. The point I am making is that this idea of endless life is there, in the history of humanity as far back as we can go. How did it come to be there? It could not simply grow of itself. There must be reason for it, ground for it, foundation in fact for it.

BURRIS JENKINS

The Daring Dream

What a wonder it is—the great fact, or hope, or daring dream, of immortality! All the more amazing if there be no truth in it—this persistent conviction that breaks out, as Browning says, in the most unexpected ways and places, "just when we are safest" in our unbelief, through "a sunset-touch, a fancy from a flowerbell, someone's death, a chorus-ending from Euripides"—this hope that surges up in a poem, a picture, a bit of music, that life does not end with the breath; that death is not just a door out of life, but a door into life.

WILLIAM PIERSON MERRILL

Spring—and Its Intimations

Days lengthen. The night is neither so long nor so cold. The sun swings in a bigger arc across the sky, and leans less to the south. These are the obvious signs, and we do not mistake them. The greenish tinge of a clear sky at sunset is not so icy as it can be at winter's depth. The Big Dipper hangs to the east of the Pole Star of an evening, not down on the horizon where it lay at the time of the winter solstice.

The signs are there to be seen. But the great sign, the one that stirs the pulse, lies closer to the heart. It is a promise, the eternal promise of spring that livens the understanding.

Yet the mystery remains, a mystery in the fact of spring. The resurgence of life is at once baffling and bolstering to our instinctive faith. And the mystery is no less inside ourselves than in the world around us; for who can deny that the tides of spring beat in the human pulse? It is something greater than mere change. It is a resurgence of belief of a new awareness of the great continuity to which we all belong.

There is a human need for the eternal question, "Why?" But with spring, the tide recedes. The fact itself overwhelms the question. It is as though the answer came in a green and flowery flood of eager new life to drown the doubt in one stupendous wave. Who can ask why when he is knee-deep in spring itself?

The earth creaks on its cold axis, the season changes, the days grow warm, and the bud bursts. Spring comes, by the stars, and we know it by a pulse beat. A new bird sings. A seed sprouts. *And we have to believe*.

ANONYMOUS

"We Are Seven"

Do you recall the exquisite poem of William Wordsworth, "We Are Seven"? A little girl, whom the poet met on his travels, described her family. Two, she said, were at Conway, and two had gone to sea. "But that means only five," replied the poet. "The other two are in the churchyard," said the eight-year-old, "but they are only twelve steps from my mother's door. Sometimes I knit my stockings and sit upon the ground and sing to them. At other times I take my porridge and eat my supper at the grave." Then she goes on to tell how Jane departed, and how John and she played around the sacred spot until, in the season when snow came, John too was forced to go and join his sister Jane. The visitor again interrupts:

> "But they are dead; those two are dead,
>   Their spirits are in heaven.
> 'Twas throwing words away, for still
>   The little maid would have her will,
>   And say, 'Nay, we are seven.'"

WILLIAM P. LEMON

Embryo Philosophers

Sir Thomas Browne put his faith in these words: "A dialogue between two infants in the womb concerning the state of this world might handsomely illustrate our ignorance of the next, whereof methinks we yet discuss in Plato's den—a cave of transitive shadows—we are but embryo philosophers." And Sir William Osler: "Some of you will wander through all phases to come at last, I trust, to the opinion of Cicero, who 'had rather be mistaken with Plato than be right with those who deny altogether a life after death,' and this is my own *Confessio Fidei.*"

THE PULPIT

The Living Light

When Augustine came to England as a missionary he was met by King Ethelbert. After the king had heard the Christian speak, he said: "All of us are like little birds that fly out of light into darkness. This man thinks he knows about the darkness to which we go. Let us listen to him." Jesus knew no diagram of heaven, but we listen attentively to him for his sure word about the mystery we so often call the darkness of the grave. He taught that death is nothing to fear; for death is but an open gate through which we journey, not to a fairer land on high, but to a lovelier life with God.

LYNN HOUGH CORSON

Miracle

Seems it strange that thou shouldst live forever? Is it less strange that thou shouldst live at all? This is a miracle; and that no more.

EDWARD YOUNG

Thoughts at a Grave

Robert G. Ingersoll, standing by his brother's grave, said: "Life is a narrow veil between the cold and barren peaks of two eternities. We strive in vain to look beyond the heights. We cry aloud, and the only answer is the echo of our wailing cry. From the voiceless lips of the unreplying dead there comes no word. But in the night of death, Hope sees a star, and listening Love can hear the rustle of a wing."

A Higher Transition

A grubworm in a pond once approached the amphibian frog and said: "Respected frog, may I ask you a question?" "Ask away," burbled the frog. "Well, what I want to know," said the water worm, "is, what's beyond the world?" "What world?" said the frog. "Why, the world of this pond we live in," said the grub. "If you think this pond is all there is, what do you call what is outside the pond?" puffed the pompous frog. "That's what I want to know," said the worm meekly. "Well, if you must know, it's dry land," said the frog. "And what's that?" said the grub. "Can you swim there?" "Why, no, of course not, you poor, ignorant worm; there is no water there." "Well, if there is no water there, then what is there?" "Why, air, of course." "Air! What is that?" That puzzled even the frog, who said: "Well, it's the nearest thing to nothing that I know of."

"I don't understand," said the grub. "That is to be expected," said the frog, and swam away. But one day the grubworm felt an irresistible urge to climb a lily stem and lie upon a lily pad, until the sun dried its skin; whereupon it split open and stepped out a dragon fly with wings of gorgeous gauze. And buzzing above the old frog, he said: "Now, I understand."

Someday we may hope to understand what is now in the nature of the case beyond our comprehension. If nature has already worked the wonder of amphibiosis, who shall say a similar but higher transition may not be made by us in the future?

ALFRED W. SWAN

Nature's Songs of Immortality

There are no proofs of immortality. No one can demonstrate, like a theorem in Euclid, that if a man dies, he shall live again. Some things are too great to be proved —God, for instance. A man wastes his breath and his time trying to prove that God is. Humanity obstinately and incurably believes in God; and you cannot prove to humanity the contrary. Emerson once said, "I am sorry if I have been betrayed into saying anything that requires proof."

The poet of the lakes, Wordsworth, however, saw keenly and far when he coined the phrase, "intimations of immortality." There are plenty of intimations all about us. Over and over again the poets, who are the truest seers, have pointed out to us the return of spring, the bursting of the buds from dead limbs, the flowers that thrust up from frost-bitten roots, the resurgence of a resistless tide of life which, with the passing of winter and its deadness, gladdens all living things with a sense of resurrection. The primrose by the river's brim, the flower in the crannied wall, the bursting eggshell, the broken chrysalis—all these are nature's poetry singing to us of unending life.

BURRIS JENKINS

Spring—Resurrection

Spring marks the smallest sparrow's flight. The increasing light draws the birds northward as, northward, the growing length of day takes its flight toward the pole.

These winging hosts, together with the flowers in the woods, bear witness innocently; like our earth, their lives are obediently inclined toward the source of light. Spring is a testament to life eternal, and a promise of the resurrection.

ANONYMOUS

A Gallant Farewell

The validity of the intimations of immortality is attested by the notable people who have felt them. The finest minds and the most sensitive souls among us have followed this instinct of immortality with a childlike faith. John Morley waves a gallant farewell as he concludes his *Book of Recollections* with these words, "So to my home and in the falling twilight." To what home did he refer? Surely no other than that promised by Jesus—"I go to prepare a place for you." . . .

Robert Louis Stevenson, that joyous and eternally youthful spirit despite his long battle with the medicine bottle, awaits the touch of death on his island in the Pacific with these brave words:

> "The breeze from the embalmèd land
>   Blows sudden toward the shore
>   And claps my cottage door. . . .
> I hear the signal, Lord,
>   I understand;
>   The night at thy command
> Comes;
> I will eat and sleep,
>   And will not question more."

NORMAN VINCENT PEALE

Flowers, Gardens, and Heaven

What is our love of flowers, our calm happiness in our gardens, but a dim recollection of our first home in paradise and a yearning for the Land of Promise!

DEAN HOLE

Life's Origin and Destiny

None of us can take life merely for what it seems to be on the surface. Deep questions arise in our hearts which we cannot escape. We keep wondering as to whence we came and whither we are going. To think in simple earnestness upon the ultimate meanings of our life is an act of worship. Such thoughts lead us at last into the presence of God, the Source and Author of our being, who reveals himself as the companion and guide of our earthly way, and who directs our footsteps toward an immortal home.

HERBERT L. WILLETT

Beyond the Sunset

I watch the sunset as I look out over the rim of the blue Pacific, and there is no mystery beyond the horizon line, because I know what there is over there. I have been there. I have journeyed in those lands. Over there where the sun is sinking is Japan. That star is rising over China. In that direction lie the Philippines. I know all that. Well, there is another land that I look forward to as I watch the sunset. I have never seen it. I have never seen anyone who has been there, but it has a more abiding reality than any of these lands which I do know. This land beyond the sunset—this land of immortality, this fair and blessed country of the soul—why, this heaven of ours is the one thing in the world which I know with absolute, unshaken, unchangeable certainty. This I know with a knowledge that is never shadowed by a passing cloud of doubt. I may not always be certain about this world; my geographical locations may sometimes become confused, but the other—that I know. And as the afternoon sun sinks lower, faith shines more clearly, and hope, lifting her voice in a higher key, sings the songs of fruition. My work is about ended, I think. The best of it I have done poorly; any of it I might have done better; but I have done it. And in a fairer land, with finer material and a better working light, I shall do a better work.

ROBERT J. BURDETTE
(*In a letter written shortly before his death*)

Man's Potentialities

The conviction of immortality is strengthened by some things we may observe about us. For instance, we stand beside "General Sherman," the largest and oldest of the Sequoia trees in California. This scarred, but unconquered, giant is at least six thousand years old. A tree may live for sixty centuries! What about man with his threescore and ten years, with powers and potentialities that dwarf the majesties of nature? When we peer out into an atmosphere alive with sound waves laden with a billion voices, when we behold our sun and its mighty planets, then go on into a universe that contains three thousand million stars, identified up to this date by the searching eye of man, with exploration just begun—we are forced to answer: "Why not? We will go on and on in a universe where millions of light years express the purpose of enduring life!"

ROBERT MERRILL BARTLETT

The Bridge Is There!

I was in San Francisco on one occasion after the two great bridges had been built. My train arrived after dark one evening, and I had to leave the city about eight the next morning. So in the early morning I went to the one place in the city from which both bridges can be seen. The Bay Bridge, spanning the beautiful harbor to Oakland, was quite clear, but the Golden Gate Bridge was invisible, completely shrouded in the early morning fog. Keenly disappointed, I waited as long as I could, as the sun rose higher, and at last I was partially rewarded. An extraordinary thing happened. The fog lifted, but only between the upright piers of the bridge, leaving the land anchorages still unseen, while the central part of the bridge, the suspension span, became clearer and clearer.

Then it was that I thought: how like our purely human view of life! We see it between the two piers, but the shore anchorages are invisible. Yet we know they must be there! Is not that a parable of immortality? So much of life as lies between the piers of birth and death we can see, as the sunlight of our mortal years re-

veals it. What lies beyond we cannot see, yet somehow
we feel with as great certainty as I felt in viewing that
bridge that there must be anchorage beyond, to which
every girder and every cable is connected, or the bridge
of life would quickly collapse into a meaningless tangle.

ELMER S. FREEMAN

Integrity of the Universe

The desire to live on after death is normal, widespread,
persistent: why not trust the integrity of the universe to
keep tryst also with this demand of human nature?

CHARLES R. BROWN

"As Dying and Behold We Live"

I had a bed of asters last summer that reached clear
across my garden in the country. How gaily they
bloomed! They were planted late. On the sides were yet
fresh blossoming flowers, while the tops had gone to
seed. Early frosts came, and I found one day that that
long line of radiant beauty was seared, and I said: "Ah!
the season is too much for them; they have perished."
And I bade them farewell.

I disliked to go and look at the bed, it looked so like
a graveyard of flowers. But, four or five weeks ago, one
of my men called my attention to the fact that along the

whole line of that bed there were asters coming up in the greatest abundance; and I looked, and behold! for every plant that I thought the winter had destroyed there were fifty plants!

What did those frosts and surly winds do? They caught my flowers, they slew them, they cast them to the ground, they trod with snowy feet upon them, and they said, leaving their work, "This is the end of you." And the next spring there were for every root fifty gloriously colorful witnesses to rise up and say, "By death we live!"

HENRY WARD BEECHER

"Hints of Occasions Infinite"

When we approach the question of immortality from the purely scientific point of view, the best we can do is to balance one set of evidence against the other and then deduce what we will—which, of course, leads us into the region of faith. It might be remembered that science itself depends upon intimations, inspirations, even faith; for, as Lord Kelvin told us long ago, when the scientist comes to the end of demonstration, he must take what he calls a mortal leap to come finally to truth. Thus, if in scientific inquiry the gleam of intimations leads the scientist on, so may we in this field have confidence in the validity and accuracy of our intimations of immortality. Thus, Lowell, in "The Cathedral," is dealing with sound doctrine when he exclaims: "We sometimes have intimations clear of wide scope, hints of occasions infinite."

NORMAN VINCENT PEALE

Standing on a Star

One night on a mountain I was looking at the stars. How vast and solid seemed the earth beneath me! How far away and tiny those glittering points of light! My imagination vainly beat its wings against infinity. I remembered the light-years by which astronomers measure the gulfs of space. I recalled the unbelievable magnitudes of Algol and Betelgeuse. Then as I thought I stood on a solid world looking at the stars of heaven, I was startled by the thought that I too was standing on a star—not a great primary star either, but a little planetary one, moving around a lesser sun. Yes, I looked at the stars, but I too lived on a star. I was afloat in the great spaces, a citizen of the skies. Then I remembered the words, "In my father's house are many mansions." I had always looked up to a heaven beyond death through the telescope of those words. They describe the heavenly home.

ARTHUR W. HEWITT

Headed for a Distant Continent

If you should discover in the tanks of an airplane only a few gallons of gasoline, you would be justified in inferring that only some such hop as from Wichita to Kansas City was contemplated. But if in the tanks you should find several hundred gallons, you would be justified in inferring that a Lindbergh was about to strike out for a distant continent. The equipment of the ship indicates a distant destination. No young animal sprouts wings except as a prophecy of flight, or fins unless it is destined to live in the water.

So with the equipment of the human spirit. "The outfit of the animal," said James Martineau, "seems an ideal provision for the purely terrestrial sphere in which it is placed, while the outfit of man, if the terrestrial sphere be all that is appointed for him, seems clearly a vast overprovision."

ALFRED W. SWAN

Ingersoll on Immortality

Immortality is a word that Hope through all the ages has been whispering to Love. The miracle of thought we cannot understand. The mystery of life and death we cannot comprehend. This chaos called world has never been explained. The golden bridge of life from gloom emerges, and on shadow rests. Beyond this we do not know. Fate is speechless, destiny is dumb, and the secret of the future has never yet been told. We love; we wait; we hope. The more we love, the more we fear. Upon the tenderest heart the deepest shadows fall. All paths, whether filled with thorns or flowers, end here.

Here success and failure are the same. The rag of wretchedness and the purple robe of power all differences and distinctions lose in this democracy of death. Character survives; goodness lives; love is immortal.

ROBERT G. INGERSOLL

"As You Will"

Not everyone, but surely the person who is committed to the life of God in Christ shall live eternally. The choice of life triumphant over death is up to you and me. An ancient story tells of a would-be cynic who, seeking to outwit a sage, held a tiny bird in his hand and asked the sage two questions. The first was, "What have I in my hand?" The sage replied, "A bird." Then the cynic, proposing to trap the sage by letting the bird fly away or by crushing it to death, and so proving the sage incorrect in either answer he might give, asked, "Is it dead or alive?" The sage replied, "As you will." So life can triumph over death, but whether your life persistently triumphs over death or not depends on your own decision.

CHARLES W. KEGLEY

PERSONALITY
IS DEATHLESS

"Thou wilt not leave us in the dust"

PERSONALITY
IS DEATHLESS

"Not Made to Die"

Thou wilt not leave us in the dust:
Thou madest man, he knows not why,
He thinks he was not made to die;
And thou hast made him: thou art just.

ALFRED TENNYSON

Personal Immortality

When I speak of immortality, I mean personal immortality, for a subpersonal or nonpersonal immortality is to me no immortality at all. The doctrine of corporate immortality is, in my judgment, a juggling with words. Losing oneself in the ocean of being, or disappearing as a conscious unit in the vast mass of created life, are speculations which do not appeal to my mind. Personality, I

am convinced, is indestructible. It is not a flame which
death can blow out. It is not an instrument or organ
which the grave can destroy. To me, the thought of extinction is abhorrent. The corpuscles in my blood re-
volt against it. My reason also repudiates it. If life ends
at the grave, the world is an insoluble mystery and God
is not a God to be worshiped or loved.

CHARLES E. JEFFERSON

He Still Lives!

In the days of my youth the commanding genius of our
part of the world was Phillips Brooks. He gave new
faith to people; he stood before thousands and uttered
such messages that we said their ultimate source was
God. The world was bright and firm in his presence. He
was at the summit of his triumphant leadership—and
then, one day, we were told that he was dead. Do you
suppose that any of us who had looked up to him believed that he was gone forever from human life? Such
a life could not suddenly be snuffed out. He is alive
somewhere in all his glorious strength.

CHARLES L. SLATTERY

When a Good Man Dies

When the sun goes below the horizon, he is not set; the
heavens glow for a full hour after his departure. And

when a great and good man dies, the sky of this world is luminous long after he is out of sight. Such a man cannot die out of this world. When he goes he leaves behind him much of himself. Being dead, he speaks.

HENRY WARD BEECHER

Life Has Value—Therefore Immortality

Why do I believe in personal immortality? Because God is God and man is man and life is what it is. Once we see what it is that gives dignity, worth, and meaning to life, argument for immortality is not needed. Until we do see it, argument is useless. Faith affirms that life has value. Religion is the realization of the value of life. Faith in immortality is faith in the conservation of the highest values of life. Since these values are personal values, faith in personal immortality is inevitable.

JOSEPH FORT NEWTON

What Death Means

The fact of death means nothing more to me than the disintegration of a body in which I am privileged to live, a body bequeathed to me from the brutes, and which has more or less adapted itself to the sort of life one must live in this world. Death means only the destruction of a house in which I live. It does not touch me. If I keep myself responsive to the lure of high and lofty ideals, if I fight hard to keep the soul on top, if when I stumble along the road I face in the right direction when I get up, if there is in me the will to be loyal to the good, the true, and the beautiful, then there will be found in me certain values which transcend the fact of death. If, in other words, I live *now* with the spirits of just men made perfect, there can be no element of moral surprise in anything which may await me beyond the incident of death. My vista of eternity comprehends all the spiritual values in the present, which will live forever, and death cannot possibly matter.

It is my hope that God means to win the game at last with every human life, that

> "Not one good shall be destroyed
>   Or cast as rubbish to the void
>   When God hath made the pile complete."

M. H. LICHLITER

The Soul's Great Adventure

Man's capacity for his highest life glows to greater flame as his fleshly habitation slowly succumbs to its ultimate decay. Corot declares at seventy-seven: "If the Lord lets me live two years longer I think I can paint something beautiful." William James, as he is going to death, says:

"I am just getting fit to live." Goethe, as he steps into the darkness, exclaims: "More light, more light."

The more truth we learn the more we are able to learn. The more goodness we see the more we are able to see. The further we go the further we are able to go. Our bodies are heir to animal decay, but our spirits are on a road with no visible terminus. We are dwelling in a world whose margin fades forever and forever as we move. Human life has what philosophers call "unexplainable overendowment" for mere physical existence.

In shallow little coves at summer resorts you have seen flat boats that children can rent for an hour. A glance will tell you that they are not intended to do more than hug the nearest shore. You may also have seen great liners like the Queen Elizabeth at an ocean port. They are different. For the moment little tugs may be pushing them into some moldy pier, but you know the time will come when they will cast off their hawsers and head out to sea. They are designed to do business in great waters.

Just so one feels about the human soul. It was made for more than the shoals and ports of time. It, like the stately ships, is designed to do business in great waters!

ERNEST MARSHALL HOWSE

Beyond Chemistry

If we should take immortality in earnest it would make a difference in what we think about ourselves. The deepest mystery in the universe is not among the stars, but

within ourselves. Some chemists with a flair for statistics
have figured that the average man is composed of chemical elements worth about ninety-eight cents. Yet this
ninety-eight cents' worth of chemical material has been
curiously put together, so that in consequence we have
some people who have immeasurably blessed our souls.
Our mothers, our saints and prophets, our great musicians,
poets, and leaders all were made of ninety-eight cents'
worth of chemical material. Immortality means this: Do
you think it is an adequate statement of the truth that
ninety-eight cents' worth of chemical material cleverly
put together by Nature, not knowing what she did,
eventuated in Isaiah, Paul, Augustine, Luther, Lincoln,
and, forgive the irreverence, in Jesus Christ himself?

HARRY EMERSON FOSDICK

No Weakling's Escape

Belief in immortality is neither a weakling's escape from
a world that he cannot master nor the dreamer's wishful
thinking. It is an affirmation of the dignity of man, of
his uniqueness among the creatures of earth, and of his
kinship to God.

"My foothold is tenoned and mortised in granite;
I laugh at what you call dissolution;
And I know the amplitude of time."

CHARLES CLAYTON MORRISON

Our Father's World

Jesus taught that this is our Father's world, and that God clothes the grass of the field and feeds the birds of the air. He also taught that personality is the most important thing in the world, worth far more than beautiful flowers, sparrows, and sheep. God made man "a little lower than the angels" and has "crowned him with glory and honor." Personality is the most valuable treasure in the universe. Through faith we are convinced that we can trust the words of Jesus concerning the home of a life beyond: "In my Father's house are many mansions: if it were not so, I would have told you. I go to prepare a place for you. And if I go and prepare a place for you, I will come again, and receive you unto myself; that where I am, there ye may be also."

CHARLES R. WOODSON

The Worth of Human Personality

Christianity affirms that man is made in the image and likeness of God and that he has within him the breath of divine life. It stresses the incalculable worth of human personality. If man has such value it is surely inconceivable that death should be the end of everything for him, that he should be blown out of existence as a candle is blown out, that he should be obliterated and annihilated. It is not only inconceivable; it is irrational. As one thinker after another has expressed the matter, if there is no other life, then this world is a stupid joke.

ROBERT J. McCRACKEN

"A Dreadful Calamity"?

In expressing his scorn of immortality George Bernard Shaw missed the point concerning the place of growth. He admitted that it would be "a dreadful calamity to have this thing named Shaw go on forever pouring out plays by the hundreds and writing books by the score." Many will agree that such would be a calamity unless "this thing named Shaw" improved in vision, depth, and outlook, and even in faith. But the likelihood is that he would improve and that his very improvement would give him a new and strange desire for immortality.

CARL KNUDSEN

Facing the Future

Some people have been able to face the future with poise and radiance. Hosts of individuals have slipped out of this world with their faces toward the sunrise. Chaucer died writing a poem. Mozart asked, as the mists gathered before his eyes, that he might hear again those harmonies that had been his life. Painters, writers, youths who have dreamed of a profession, and then were blown to bits by a bursting shell, have felt that they were only beginning their lifework when death came. Are such personalities to be thrown on the ash heap simply out of deference to the dissolution of a few particles of matter? Surely the things which are unseen are the most real "things" in our lives! If we can believe this, we have a faith that lights up the heavens in the blackout of doubt.

G. RAY JORDAN

Not a Shadow of Uncertainty

Walter Russell Bowie, rector of Grace Protestant Episcopal Church, New York, tells the story of Wilbur Cosby Bell, professor in Virginia Theological Seminary. Dr. Bell was dying after a sudden illness of only a few hours. He sent this message to the boys he had taught in the seminary: "Tell the boys that I've grown surer of God every year of my life, and I've never been so sure as I am right now. I am so glad to find that I haven't the least shadow of shrinking or uncertainty. I have always thought so and now that I am right up against it, I know. Life owes me nothing. I've had work that I loved, and I've lived in a beautiful place among congenial friends. I've had love in its highest form and I've got it forever. I can see now that death is just the smallest thing, just an accident, but it means nothing. There is no real break, and life, all that really counts in life, goes on." So he passed, he who had always lived with the spirits of just men made perfect, and all the trumpets sounded for him on the other side.

M. H. LICHLITER

The Universal Hope

That there is a life beyond death is one of the most universal convictions of the human race. Sociologists report that it is more widespread even than belief in a God or gods. Men have difficulty in reconciling themselves to a theory involving their own ultimate extinction. Their hope of immortality is intuitive and inbred. The intellect, the heart, the conscience demand it. There is an undiscourageable, inextinguishable assurance in man, rooted in something which he feels is of the very essence of his being, that death cannot be the end.

ROBERT J. MCCRACKEN

Old Age and Immortality

If there are parts of life in which we grow old, are there other parts in which we can stay young? Are there other realms in which a genuine youthfulness may persist throughout the years? One day when John Quincy Adams was eighty years of age a friend met him on the streets of Boston. "How is John Quincy Adams?" this friend asked gaily. The old man's eyes began to twinkle, and then he spoke slowly. His words have become classic. "John Quincy Adams himself is very well, thank you. But the house he lives in is sadly dilapidated. It is tottering on its foundations. The walls are badly shattered, and the roof is worn. The building trembles with every wind, and I think John Quincy Adams will have to move out of it before long. But he himself is very well." And with a wave of the hand the old man walked on. Was he old or young? Old in body but astonishingly young in spirit. That was his victory over the years, a victory which was only partial but was still indubitably real. He had learned to stay young as he grew old.

JAMES GORDON GILKEY

Personality Is Never Destroyed

My most convincing human reason for belief in immortality is personality. Nothing is ever annihilated. No form of life ever dies without some form of resurrection. The oak has its acorn, and for every sunset there is a sunrise. Forms may change but life itself moves with a tide as irresistible as the recurring seasons. Personality may change its residence and lay aside the flesh that clothed it, but never is destroyed.

But immeasurably beyond reason, is faith: that faith in which we declare, "I know whom I have believed and I am persuaded that he is able to keep that which I have committed unto him against that day."

DANIEL A. POLING

No Regrets

What George Herbert Palmer wrote about the death of his wife, Alice Freeman Palmer, has become a classic:

"Though no regrets are proper for the manner of her death, who can contemplate the fact of it and not call the world irrational if, out of deference to a few particles of disordered matter, it excludes so fair a spirit?"

WILLIAM PIERSON MERRILL

"In the Father's House"

Arthur John Gossip, great Scottish preacher, lost his wife in the early twenties of this century. In 1929, when he published a volume of sermons, he surprised the world by dedicating it: "To My Wife—My Daily Comrade Still." The sequel to this is even more beautiful. In 1945, twenty years after her death, he issued another volume of sermons, dedicating it: "To My Wife—Now a Long Time in the Father's House."

K. MORGAN EDWARDS

Immortal Youth

The more we sink into the infirmities of age, the nearer we are to immortal youth. All people are young in the other world. That state is an eternal spring, ever fresh and flourishing. Now, to pass from midnight into noon on the sudden; to be decrepit one minute and all spirit and activity the next, must be a desirable change. To call this dying is an abuse of language.

JEREMY TAYLOR

Victory in Death

Dr. S. Parkes Cadman was one of the greatest souls who ever graced a pulpit in America. Massive in thought and with a heart as big as the world, he poured out his soul in platform deliverances of rare spiritual power. He was sympathetic toward the humblest brother Christian who sought his counsel or only his friendliness.

In his fatal illness this great preacher of the gospel was rushed to a hospital. His suffering was intense and prolonged, but through it all he was absolutely triumphant. Not once did he lose his kindliness toward those who served him; not once did his radiance and fortitude fail him; not once did he lose his buoyancy of spirit. When others wept, he steadied them with his quiet trust. His eternal nature was already asserting his victory over the flesh. When the great transition had been made, a nurse exclaimed, "Never in all my life have I seen anyone like him!"

CARL KNUDSEN

Reverence for Personality

It is upon the Christian conviction of human worth—reverence for personality—that we build our hope of the life everlasting. Quite true, man dies physically as the animal dies. But there is something in man different, and it makes him different, from the lower creation. He is a spiritual being, and this changes the whole outlook.

When I see man at his best—flowering forth in a Moses, a Socrates, or a Jesus—then I say he ought to live on. And because he ought, he will. It is inconceivable that the universe would produce such a superb being and then suddenly strike him down, thrusting him into eternal oblivion. With John Fiske, "I believe in the immortality of the soul as a supreme act of faith in the reasonableness of God's work."

J. J. CASTLEBERRY

What Is Man!

Call not man "the quintessence of dust." Forget his baseness. Behold the stars, the untold treasures of the soul. What a rise this is, from protoplasm to Plato! Today a babe, tomorrow a Shakespeare! Today a feeble cry, tomorrow the mighty voice of Luther! Today a lip on a mother's breast, tomorrow the eloquence of Paul! Thus a few years can raise man from nothingness to grandeur, from a cradle to Olympus, from dust to divinity. And has ever a life exhausted the possibilities of the soul?

ANDREAS BARD

Not a Question of Quantity

In the interesting fantasy, *Lost Horizon*, by James Hilton, we find Hugh Conway talking to the High Lama of the Tibetan Monastery. The old man explains that due to the physical conditions, the elimination of struggle, and emphasis upon beauty and peace, men live many years. He himself is 250 years old. Conway replies that he is not interested in just prolonging life unless it has a purpose. "I've sometimes doubted whether life itself has any point and, if not, long life must be even more pointless." Then the Lama tells him that he wishes him to be his successor and to guard the treasures of the age so that after the catastrophe of world disorder, he can help rebuild better.

Eternal life according to Christ was not a question of quantity, but of quality. It was more than a mere extension of time. He promises it not in the future but now. Into the present life he brings deathless values. If the present life is meaningless, why prolong it? Jesus bids us live now "by the power of an endless life." Raymond Calkins says that a man should ask himself, "Can I think of my life lasting forever in its present terms? How much of my life, my interests, my character, deserves immortality?"

A. E. COWLEY

In a Friendly Universe

I do not think there is sufficient evidence at hand in the scientific sense to prove that the dead live. Someday that may come. For the present, believing in a universe at once orderly and friendly, I cannot think of personality as snuffed out just at the moment when one begins to see, even if it be through a glass darkly. Great souls about

me must live. I cannot reason out immortality. My soul
craves it, and somehow I feel that a Father God, having
builded a universe wherein urgent desires have the possibility of satisfaction, will satisfy this one.

G. BROMLEY OXNAM

The Dead Are the Living

Life is life forever! To be is eternal being. Every man
that has died is at this instant in full possession of all his
faculties, in the intensest exercise of all his capacities,
standing somewhere in God's great universe, ringed with
a sense of God's presence, and feeling in every fiber of
his being that life which comes after death is not less real
but more real, not less great but more great, not less full
and intense but more full and intense, than the mingled
life which, lived here on earth, was a center of life surrounded with a crust and circumference of mortality.
The dead are the living. They lived while they died,
and after they die they live on forever.

ALEXANDER MACLAREN

Why a Future Existence?

Grievous the loss to justice through the decline of faith
in immortality. "Shall not the Judge of all the earth do
right?" has been a question asked by good men for thousands of years.

One of the hardest problems the human intellect has to solve is the fact that in this life the bravest patriots, the wisest teachers, the noblest leaders of humanity, have lived in huts, worn rags, and eaten crusts. Here, through fidelity to their great convictions, they have struggled for years to hold heartbreak at bay. But if there is no summerland beyond where all these cruel wrongs are righted, then surely life would not be worth living!

The great, creative personality has oft been lonely and neglected in his day, but beyond, "he shall find his natural associates and lovers, and hear the chorus of that great company that give him greeting and gratitude in the moment that his eyes close upon the world of matter that now is."

NEWELL DWIGHT HILLIS

Here—and There

Here and now, our misfortune is irreparable. Our service to others is limited. Our thirst for larger activity is unsatisfied. The greatest workers for the race are at times shaken with a mighty cry of the soul, a longing more fully to body forth the energy, the fire, the richness of fancy and of human impulse which overburden them. What wonder, then, that we with our more limited senses and more humble powers should with a passionate desire crave wider range and scope of usefulness!

HELEN KELLER

In a Rational Universe

The belief in immortality is as natural to man as are hunger, thirst, and breath. It has persisted through the ages. It is a conviction which rests upon the very integrity of the universe. When we survey the long and costly course personality has traveled, the belief in immortality is inescapable. Something abiding must come of personality after death, or else the whole creative process of life is utterly purposeless. If life ended at the grave, this would be an irrational universe. It is impossible to believe that God, having brought forth his highest creation—human personality—through the travail of millions of years, will toss it aside as an unimportant experiment.

CHARLES R. WOODSON

Law of the Spirit of Life

A French deist argues at length with a Christian friend against immortality. The friend replies in a sentence: "Probably you are right. I presume you are not immortal; but I am." He has expressed in that sentence the foundation of my own faith in immortality. Immortality is in a true sense a present fact. I *am* immortal now; not merely shall be; though the "shall be" is projected into the future necessarily out of the "I am." The immortal nature is within; and I feel its strivings, as the unfledged bird the growing power of flight before he spreads his wings and launches from his nest upon the invisible and untried element on which without a fear he trusts himself.

LYMAN ABBOTT

Immortality Required

The best men and their purposes in life require immortality, and if they do not get it, the universe is cheated if it is not a cheat. Take the case of Jesus. His character is of a sort that seems indestructible. The universe would seem morally wrong if purposes like those of Jesus did not get a fair chance. By precisely the same token, other persons with such purposes deserve immortality for the fulfillment of those purposes. Such "best men" and such as Jesus need forever!

WILLIAM F. McDOWELL

For Those Who Are Worthy of It

I have found, as a matter of experience, that arguments in favor of immortality do not convince disbelievers in it; but rather tend to harden them in their opposition to it—at least that is the case with philosophical arguments. I am inclined to think that belief in immortality does not require much public profession, and is more likely to arise when it is left to private conviction. I believe, myself, in the survival of the human personality after the death of the body for those who are worthy of it. About those who are not worthy of it, and there are such, I am by no means so confident.

L. P. JACKS

What Are You Going to Do About It?

I write you from my small hospital vessel, of which I am captain, on the badly charted, icebound coast of Labrador, where for the past months we have had nothing but winds and fogs. You can see I live in a world where preconceived opinions are at a discount, for one too often finds by action how valueless they are.

What interests me most about personal immortality is, "What am I going to do about it?" The only intellectual satisfaction I expect my brain to grasp concerning reality has been attained in the way the Master of men told us we could expect it. He says: "The light of life comes to those who follow me in action the best they know how." My experience confirms my intuition that the beauty and the glory of what we call life here need not be of necessity a loathsome tragedy. My intense desire for life is a natural and not an artificial one. I have not had to stand by deathbeds for forty years and not know how universal that desire is in the normal human being.

The truth is, I have not any "opinion" about personal immortality. I am as certain of it as I am that I get a new skin every month.

WILFRED T. GRENFELL

On the Seas of God

In our daily lives, we constantly take for granted what men once said was impossible. Who shall say that those who dedicate themselves to the absolute in integrity, the positive in love, the ultimate in hope, and dwell in like spiritual essence with God, may not cry out at the last, "O death, where is thy sting, and grave thy victory?" So let us

"Steer forth—steer for the deep waters only,
Are they not all the seas of God?"

SAMUEL HARKNESS

Life in God Cannot Die

When life is lived with God in Christ it cannot end or be defeated. If your life expresses the purposes and shares the spirit of God, it cannot conclude with death or disaster. Life in God triumphs over death, because God's life knows not defeat or death. "Whosoever liveth and believeth in me shall never die."

CHARLES W. KEGLEY

Human Personality—and God

My belief in a continuation of conscious personal existence after the disintegration of the flesh is based on religious grounds, which do not seem to me to be negatived by anything objected to by physical science or biology. My religious belief rests on the conviction that human personality can and does come into relations of filial dependence on a Personality that directs the universe along lines of wisdom and goodness.

BENJAMIN W. BACON

In a Moral Order

Manifestly the soul is as immortal as the moral order which inhabits it, else morality were a mockery. Frail we are, and fleeting, but in their outworking the laws of the moral and spiritual life reach far beyond life and time and death, and become prophets of a life that shall endless be.

JOSEPH FORT NEWTON

FEAR DEATH?
THERE IS NO DEATH!

Even Science Declares That Nothing Dies

FEAR DEATH?
THERE IS NO DEATH!

"Another, Sadder Name for Life"

There is no death—the thing that we call death
Is but another, sadder name for life,
Which is itself an insufficient name,
Faint recognition of that unknown Life—
That Power whose shadow is the Universe.

RICHARD HENRY STODDARD

There Is No Death

There is no death! So speaks our latest and best science,
and so spake Jesus. This truth lives as comfort and help
to all men, forever. Of this eternal life, Jesus was the
first fruit. He lives, in the vast pageant of human history. He lives in the comradeship of struggling souls. He
lives in the mighty heritage of liberating truth. He lives!

49

The excellent does become the permanent. This is the victory that overcometh the world. Death hath no more dominion over him. And because he lives, you too shall live. There is no death!

BERNARD C. CLAUSEN

Is Immortality a Delusion?

If there is no life immortal, then much that is vital in religion must be discarded. If the dead be not raised, then ours is a dead Christ. We must also surrender our belief in God as "Our Father" as revealed by Christ. Life, too, has an ignoble destiny. If immortality is a delusion it is the most inspiring delusion that ever possessed the human breast. It has wiped away more tears, inspired more courage, radiated more sunshine, and kindled more hope in dreary lives than any other expectation whatsoever. "I believe in the life everlasting," because it is more credible than any alternative whatsoever.

JAMES E. CROWTHER

Love Stronger Than Death

Love is imperishable. And love is stronger than death. Time and space are powerless to destroy it. In its nature it is, like God himself, immortal. When W. R. Matthews, the dean of St. Paul's Cathedral in London, broadcast four talks on immortality, he received from listeners some 1,900 letters. About them he commented: "If there is any lesson to be learned from the letters I have had, it is that love is the main source of the desire for life beyond death." The greatest grief of life is the parting of friends, and where a life has been entwined with that of another, the grief beggars description. Love is oneness and cannot endure separation; it refuses to believe that the separation can be permanent. Robert Browning grounded his faith in immortality on the imperishableness of love. After the death of his wife he wrote:

"O thou soul of my soul! I shall clasp thee again.
And with God be the rest."

ROBERT J. McCRACKEN

Life's Candle Does Not Go Out

Sir Arthur Keith was one of the great British scientists. Professor Arthur Compton is one of the great American scientists. The first was an utter disbeliever; the second is a thorough believer. According to Sir Arthur Keith, when a man dies he goes out like a candle: to which Professor Compton replies that the candle does not go out; its energy goes on and on to the farthest reaches of the universe. Be sure of this: If God *is*, one way or another our candle does not go out. Its mode of going on may be utterly different from anything we have pictured it to be. Indeed, I am sure that must be so, but one way or another, as Emerson said,

". . . What is excellent
As God lives, is permanent,"

and in manners and fashions beyond our power to imagine, the candle does not go out.

HARRY EMERSON FOSDICK

Why Fear Death?

Men fear death as children fear to go in the dark; and as that natural fear in children is increased with tales, so is the other. Certainly the contemplation of death as the wages of sin, and passage to another world, is holy and religious; but the fear of it, as a tribute due unto nature, is weak. . . . The Stoics bestowed too much cost upon death, and by their great preparations made it appear more fearful. It is as natural to die as to be born.

SIR FRANCIS BACON

No Dread of Death for the Christian

There are people today who dread death, though sometimes I think there are more who dread life. These two things are tied together. If a man dreads death, he dreads it because he fears the unknown, since he has no clear sense of the reality of an existence which is independent of the flesh in which, and for which, he has mainly lived. The same man may come to dread life, for life's outward accidents have made it bitter to his taste, and he has no inner spiritual resources to give him strength and joy whatever the weather of his world may be. But for the Christian there is no dread of death, for it is simply the entrance into a larger room of that life which finds its security in God, in the same God from whom has come all that is sweet and sound in our living here. And for the same reason the Christian cannot despair of life. However its music may seem to be, he is sure that if he is faithful, all its notes will fit someday into a harmony that shall make its meaning great.

WALTER RUSSELL BOWIE

An Indian's Interpretation

Eternal life—there is no end to it! It is life without end. The government was trying to make a treaty with the Indians, and in one place put the word "forever." The Indians did not like that word "forever," and said: "No; put it, 'as long as water runs and grass grows.'" The Indians could understand that.

DWIGHT L. MOODY

No Death, Says the Biologist

When the biologist finds no break between my life and all of life which has gone before, he not only concludes that everything that has gone before is a part of me; he also attests that I am a part of all that comes after me.

What my life does, counts in the eternal struggle of up-reaching life. If I am beastly, I push life back toward the beast. If I am Christlike, I draw life toward his life. This life of mine, for better or worse, goes on, in all of life forever. What Christian could ask more than this from the biologist? In the deepest sense—there is no death!

BERNARD C. CLAUSEN

A Scientist on Immortality

In spite of his physical insignificance, man as an intelligent person is of extraordinary importance in the cosmic scheme. If we were to use our own best judgment, what would we say is the most important thing about a noble man? Would it be the strength of his body, or the brilliance of his intellect? Would we not place first the beauty of his character? A man's body is at its prime before middle life, and his intellect probably somewhat after middle life. But it takes a whole lifetime to build the character of a noble man. The exercise and discipline of youth, the struggles and failures and successes, the pains and pleasures of maturity, the loneliness and tranquillity of age—these make up the fire through which he must pass to bring out the pure gold of his soul. Having been thus perfected, what shall Nature do with him? Annihilate him? What infinite waste!

Speaking, now, not as a scientist but as man to man, how can a father who loves his children choose to have them die? As long as there is in heaven a God of Love, there must be for God's children everlasting life. This is not the cold logic of science but the warm faith of a father who has seen his child on the brink of death.

> "And so, at last, it may be you and I
> In some far realm of blue infinity
> Shall find together some enchanted shore
> Where Life and Death and Time shall be no more,
> Leaving Love only and Eternity."
>
> ARTHUR H. COMPTON

Life First, Then Immortality

Christianity is concerned more with life than with immortality. St. Paul employs the word "immortality" only twice. The great Christian word is "life," not "soul." While immortality suggests an immunity to death, resurrection emphatically affirms the re-creation of man through death. Dying to live—that is the thought that streams through the fabric and faith of Christianity. Nature itself reveals this fact: In dying, the seed lives. So, in dying, man lives. It is the law of life.

GEORGE McNEILL RAY

Meeting Death Unafraid

We cannot evade death if we would. We should not wish to, even if we might. Those who have lived in close and habitual familiarity with spiritual things seem to find death wearing a familiar and friendly countenance when they meet him face to face. They make ready for his coming with quiet hope and faith, and often they ask us who remain not to mourn their departure as though we had been robbed of their presence. They but go a little way ahead of us, and await us around the bend. The soul that has learned to face duty from day to day is ever prepared to meet death unafraid.

HERBERT L. WILLETT

When Hope Goes—Flowers

Where our death seems to be, there our Saviour is. Where the end of hope is, there is the brightest beginning of fruition. Where the darkness is thickest, there the bright beaming light that never is set is about to emerge. When the whole experience is consummated, then we find that a garden is not disfigured by a sepulcher. Our joys are made better if there be sorrow in the midst of them. And our sorrows are made bright by the joys that God has planted around about them. The flowers may not be pleasing to us, they may not be such as we are fond of plucking, but they are heart flowers, love, hope, faith, joy, peace—these are flowers which are planted about every grave that is sunk in the Christian heart.

ANONYMOUS

The Grave As Viewed by Christians

Our soul is not really brave unless it can face the facts
of life in the revealing light that death throws upon them.
For death is a fact, a fact which we observe all about us,
and a fact which each one of us must someday experience. Without the slightest taint of morbidness or
alarm or false piety it is profitable for us to stand apart
from life now and then, and assess its values as we shall
assess them someday when we meet death face to face.
From such a point of view much that is now important
would seem negligible, while many things we are now
neglecting would take on urgent and eternal values.

HERBERT L. WILLETT

Death Is a Servant, Not a Master

Many of us, as time goes on, cease to believe the doctrine
of the immortality of the soul. Let me advise you what
you ought to do if that happens to you. If you can possibly help it, do not talk about your views. Be patient:
you may change your mind again, before you die. Keep,
in a quiet way, to the usual observances of your religion:
be content to be conventional, be content to be incon-
sistent. Almost all of us arrive at these views: and some
remain there, and some do not. Your duty is to wait.
Possibly, nothing will come of your waiting: possibly,
something. It may be, for you, a matter of holding on
with patience, and of recognizing what great evidences,

authorities, and examples are on the side of this doctrine. And, whatever may come, or not come, of your long waiting, always be sure of one fact, that Death is a servant, having a Master over him: as the inscription at Zermatt says, over a man killed by an avalanche: It is I, be not afraid. Death beats his drum, this way and that, in the crowd of our lives; he is doing what he was told: and I hope that I shall thus think of him when he comes to me.

STEPHEN PAGET

Death Swallowed Up in Victory

Man's state on this earth is marked by corruption and mortality. We actually live a dying life, yet we carry all the while the eternal seed of our immortality. "We shall all be changed, in a moment, in the twinkling of an eye . . . for this corruptible must put on incorruption, and this mortal must put on immortality . . . death is swallowed up in victory." "But to God thanks, to him who gives to us the victory through Jesus Christ our Lord."

Paul must have anticipated the immeasurable delight in the promised release from his earthly infirmities, from the innumerable sufferings to which his mind and body were subjected even unto death. No wonder Paul sang! No wonder the Christians down through the ages have joined in the triumphant chorus! No wonder we offer thanks to God for this victory!

GEORGE McNEILL RAY

Why Be Afraid?

O frail child of the dust, yet mighty son of eternity, why
be afraid? You are life itself: august, unfathomable, supreme, tremendous! Death is your humble servant, not
master. Since you are life, how can you die? And since
death is your servant, why fear your helper? Lift up
your head; fling wide your hopes; dare greatly; grasp
heroically the reins of destiny, and with one mighty leap
of the heart cry in exaltation that all the world may hear
—"I am not afraid!"

ANONYMOUS

Science and Immortality

What thought so inevitably leaps to the mind in April,
the month of Easter, as the thought of immortality? The
imagery and the language in which that thought clothes
itself have changed with the changing thoughts of men
and their enlarging knowledge of the universe, but the
thought itself is as immortal as man himself. It is as
irrepressible as the sprouting seed whose tender but in-
domitable shoot pushes its way among the stones and
gropes through darkness to the light. Science has en-
larged the temporal and spatial scale by which the material universe is measured, from hundreds to billions of
miles, from a few thousand to hundreds of millions of
years, so that the stage of our human life seems shrunk
to a point and its duration to a moment in the midst of

incalculable immensities. "Up" and "down" lost their meaning when the world ceased to be flat, and the seeker for a heaven just above the clouds lost his sense of direction. Then science turned in upon itself and discovered that matter is not the crude stuff that it seemed, and that this "too, too solid world" is not solid at all, but the manifestation of forces which may, after all, be better called spiritual than material. Still, science cannot prove immortality. It can only leave a place for it among the things that it can neither prove nor disprove. Within that area of liberty, men may, with no sacrifice of intellectual respectability, find room for the assertion of that quality of human personality which is the postulate of immortality.

CHARLES CLAYTON MORRISON

DAWN!

Death Marks a New Beginning

DAWN!

"The Night Behind Me"

You say, "Where goest thou?" I cannot tell,
And still go on. If but the way be straight
I cannot go amiss: before me lies
Dawn and the day: the night behind me: that
Suffices me: I break the bounds: I see,
And nothing more; believe and nothing less.

ROBERT BROWNING

Dawn!

The most impressive inscription I have ever seen upon a monument is this one word—Dawn. The monument is just above Trafalgar Square, in Charing Cross, London. There, right in the center of the busy street, stands the nation's grateful tribute to Nurse Edith Cavell. One sees a life-size figure of the nurse against a background of granite. Underneath the figure of the nurse one reads these words cut in stone:

EDITH CAVELL
Brussels
DAWN
October 12, 1915

Name, place, date, and one word—Dawn. What more need be said? All faith and hope and love are contained in the one word. Dawn—a new day, a new chance, a new idea, a new life! All this Christ brings us by way of the Easter dawn.

BRUCE S. WRIGHT

Toward the Eternal Sunrising

Man has always built the house of his hope toward the eternal sunrising. To be sure, all kinds of curious and impossible things have been believed, and we have added our full share of oddities to the record of man's striving after immortality; we have been guilty of materializing what we call heaven with our visions of golden streets and pearly gates and white-clothed angels plucking at the strings of celestial harps. We cannot do otherwise than seek to define what is beyond our experience in terms of things we know. That we have all thus striven after a knowledge and certainty is not to be doubted;

and if we picture certainty in terms not intellectually acceptable, that does not lessen at all the urgency of our search. Instinctively we feel that there is some value in man's life that does not deserve to die, and we share this feeling with the whole of humanity.

LYNN HOUGH CORSON

A New Beginning

Death is not the end; it is only a new beginning. Death is not the master of the house; he is only the porter at the King's lodge, appointed to open the gate and let the King's guests into the realm of eternal day. And so shall we ever be with the Lord.

The range of our threescore years and ten is not the limit of our life. Our life is not a landlocked lake enclosed within the shore lines of seventy years. It is an arm of the sea. And so we must build for those larger waters. We are immortal! How, then, shall we live today in prospect of eternal tomorrow?

J. H. JOWETT

New Surprises for the Soul

We are not doomed citizens of a dead universe! Rather, we are living citizens of a living universe. To live unendingly in such a universe, a universe so varied and complex, could only give lure and fascination to personal existence. Our minds cannot exhaust the wonders of the physical world which is unfolding. Is there any physicist who has exhausted his field of inquiry? No; he knows that he has only touched the border of matter, has only grasped the elementary truths of his field. Is there any musician who has exhausted the possibilities of musical expression? No; the master musician dies knowing that he has received only a preliminary training in the art of music. The life beyond acquires added attraction as we realize that this vast and unexplored universe is to be our home; that the God who planned the miracle of the atom has planned new surprises for the mind.

LLOYD ELLIS FOSTER

A Great Way to Die

G. K. Chesterton said of Robert Louis Stevenson that "he died with a thousand stories in his heart." That's a great way to die. It is a great way to live. It raises the multiplication table to its highest use, the multiplication of life.

THE PULPIT

Death a Gateway

There is a touching incident which Ramsay MacDonald tells in his exquisite memoir of his wife, whose spirit seemed ever to hover over the great English prime minister. It is the account of her passing into the spirit world. "Her faith stood the test to the end. When she knew that she was close by the opening gateway of death, I asked her if she desired to see anyone who would speak to her of what was to come. 'That would be a waste of time,' she replied. 'I have always been ready. Let us praise God together for what has been. He has been very good to me in giving me my work, my friends, and my faith. At the end of the day I go gladly to him for rest and shelter.' She was convinced that life and time were not the sum and substance of experience, and went away as though but starting on a journey which, beginning in darkness, would proceed through light. He would hold her hand, she said, till those who had gone before had her greetings."

PAUL B. KERN

The Gate of Life

Death is the servant of life. "Death," said an old Latin proverb, "is the gate of life." It comes with shadowed face, but it opens doors for life above and beyond it. If nothing ever passed away, how would the new find room or foothold? If old forms, like buried seeds, were not dissolved, how would the life-germ at the heart of them be set free? The outworn, in everything, becomes a hindrance. The garments of mortality grow old. "Come," says Death, and his voice is kind and his shad-

owed face is tender, "take them off, there are new ones
waiting. I am only a servant. Life and love are my masters, but they cannot reclothe even a buried seed—except it die."

GAIUS GLENN ATKINS

If Life Is Infinite—

If life is infinite, then it is infinite not only in duration
but in compass, in what it includes; every family on
earth and in heaven must be included in the calculation;
and the great cloud of witnesses must be reckoned as interested participants in our earthly race. Then may you
build a home and take time to build your life into it,
cementing it with cares and anxieties and tears and heart-
aches, for they too are a part of this infinite possession
of life.

On any other interpretation of life than this the great
sacrifices of history are contradictions and illusions. On
any other ground I do not know what to say about Socrates going to his death; it seems like an awful waste of a
splendid life. On any other ground I do not know how
to interpret Gethsemane and Calvary. The cross seems
to be the symbol of misjudged and misguided zeal. But
if we can raise all these terms of life to the nth power, if
we can think of it all as part of the eternal and infinite
process, then we begin to understand what Jesus meant
when he said, "If I be lifted up I will draw all men unto

me." The cross begins to symbolize, not the utter waste of life, but the gathering up of its fragments under the law of love.

With such an interpretation of life—that it is infinite—do we not begin to understand the great and solemn mystery of death which so invades our life and cuts short the thread, interrupts the tasks just begun, makes the hand stiff and cold that was just beginning to create; stops the active mind that was so eager to explore? It all seems so perplexing; it is so unless we think of life as infinite. Then we can say:

> "Our times are in His hand
> Who saith, 'A whole I planned
> Youth shows but half; trust God; see all, nor
> be afraid!'
>
> "My times be in thy hand!
> Perfect the cup as planned!
> Let age approve of youth and death complete
> the same!"

FREDERIC E. DEWHURST

"Only a Forward Step"

I remember a quiet summer evening many years ago when I sat and talked on serious themes with Ormond, of Princeton, that philosopher of massive intellect, of great heart and devout Christian beliefs. And he said to me: "The next life is only a forward step in spiritual evolution. There will probably be many stages beyond that. But never again, I believe, the shock and wrench of what we call death. Both my philosophy and my Christian belief have led me to the conviction that evolution does not stop at the present stage of development, but that it moves on in the field of the spirit as we have seen it move up within the confines of earthly experience."

Well, Ormond has moved on. He may not know all about it yet, but he knows more about it than do we. And when a great soul like that passes out through the shadows, there are "many voices crying, 'Hail.'"

CHARLES F. WISHART

The Search

We have all eternity to learn God in; it would be a poor prospect if we could get very far in our lesson here. We must expect to be puzzled and baffled again and again; only do not let us get impatient, and weary of the search, or feel tempted to think that he is nowhere because we cannot yet reach to the height of his vision.

ANNIE KEARY

Death Not the Final Word

The persistence with which we keep asking about immortality is one of the most convincing proofs of the reality of the future life. Our soul cannot adjust itself to the view that life is exhausted in the narrow ranges of our earthly adventure. Although we no longer regard this world as essentially bad, and this life as a dreary pilgrimage, yet our most optimistic estimate of our finite experience leaves our soul unsatisfied. We cannot believe that after all the achievement and tragedy of our mortal years, death is to have the final word.

HERBERT L. WILLETT

Not the End, But the Beginning

In that stirring melodrama, "The Iron Mask," there is a thrill at the conclusion. D'Artagnan, having carried his arduous and loyal task to a triumphant conclusion only to be foully dealt a fatal blow, staggers out to die alone; and then the clouds part, and one sees his three daunt-less comrades smiling down at him, and reaching down to welcome him to the new life; and on the screen flashes not the conventional word "End," but the startling word "Beginning."

Call that sentimental, if you will; and one does smile at the incongruity of the warriors marching into heaven with their swords flashing. But I am sorry for anyone who cannot see the reality under all that. The significant thing is not the bright blade, but the bright spirit, the dauntless loyalty and courage. If all that could be brought to an end by a cowardly stab in the back, then life is of little account.

WILLIAM PIERSON MERRILL

Training for Eternity

If there is no life beyond the grave, if there is no immortality, if all spiritual calculation is to end here, why, then, the mighty work of God is all to end in nothingness: but if this is only a state of infancy, only the education for eternity, in which the soul is to gain its wisdom and experience for higher work, then to ask why a loved one is taken from us is just as absurd as to question why the tree of the forest has its first training in the nursery garden. This is but the nursery ground, from whence we are to be transplanted into the great forest of God's eternal universe.

FREDERICK W. ROBERTSON

Endless Progress Ahead

God will allow no talent to perish. To every seed he will give a plant, to every acorn an oak. And like an eternal dawn after a brief twilight appears eternity with its promises of endless progress, of revelations which "eye hath not seen and ear hath not heard."

ANDREAS BARD

The View Beyond

Life is most interesting to people who have won their first view of that world which lies beyond this world of knowledge, truth, and adventure. It must have been zestful to Beethoven who after producing one of his compositions said: "My Ninth Symphony is but an empty echo of the heavenly music I heard in my dream." Or to Raphael who after painting the Sistine Madonna complained that he could not put on canvas the vision which his soul saw. Or to Isaac Newton who after his epoch-making scientific discoveries testified: "I seem to have been like a boy playing on the seashore while the great ocean of truth lay all undiscovered before me."

CARL KNUDSEN

Only a Night's Sleep

What is our death but a night's sleep? For as through sleep all weariness and faintness pass away and cease, and the powers of the spirit come back again, so that in the morning we arise fresh and strong and joyous, so at the Last Day we shall rise again as if we had only slept a night, and shall be fresh and strong.

MARTIN LUTHER

The Bright Side of Death's Separation

No treasures that we gather in our earthly adventure are comparable to the friendships, the loves, that grow up beside us during the years. It is the breaking of these companionships that gives to life its chief element of pathos. In taking away one who is dear to us, death seems to carry off a part of our essential self, and so leaves us bewildered in the midst of our familiar environment. But is not this the beginning of our orientation in the Unseen, our introduction to the mysteries with which we are to live forever? When at last our whole self is carried hence we shall awake to find heaven so familiar.

HERBERT L. WILLETT

Christianity a Morning Faith

Dawn—a new day, a new chance, a new idea, a new life. All this Christ brings us by way of the Easter dawn. There is a story about a man who was talking with Thomas Carlyle, telling him that he proposed to start a new religion which would entirely supplant the religion of Christ. There would be no mysteries about it, it would be as plain as the multiplication table. He would call the new religion "Positivism." Carlyle is said to have replied: "Good. All you will need to do now will be to speak as never man spake, live as he lived, die as he died, be crucified, rise again the third day, and get the world to believe that you are still alive; then your new religion will have a chance." In other words, all he needed to do was to put Dawn into his religion. But man cannot do that; only God can do that. "It began to dawn." There are many things we do not know; "we see through a glass darkly." But of one thing we are certain: that ours is a morning faith, that those who with faith face the tomb see an eternal sunrise.

BRUCE S. WRIGHT

Not Mere Endlessness

"Eternal" is not to be taken primarily in a quantitative sense, to signify mere endlessness. It is rather a life of new dimensions, life raised to new capacities—the full opening out of life Godward. By birth from above, the soul partakes of the life of God and enters upon a type of life as inexhaustible as his life is and as incapable of being ended by physical catastrophe.

RUFUS M. JONES

Not the End of the Trail

In one of our eastern cities is a famous statue of an Indian on a horse, called "The End of the Trail." The horse stands with drooping head at the end of the trail of life, but the Indian sits with hands and face raised toward the sky where dwells the Great Spirit in the Happy Hunting Ground. The end of the trail? Through Easter, God answers, "No!" Rather it is the beginning of the trail. It is the Christian insight and faith that everlasting life is the gift of God both here and now and then.

JOHN G. SIMMONS

The End Is the Beginning

Of all the biographies that have come from the presses, I know none that has a more fitting conclusion than E. S. Martin's *Life of Joseph H. Choate*. He tells of certain quiet words Mr. Choate spoke concerning his faith in a life beyond, and then says: "All this suggests that having lived long as life goes, and done what he could, and got what he might, he felt that what he had got and done and been was not enough, and that further adventures lay before him. One writes 'the end' of his biography, but that means only the end of a book."

WILLIAM PIERSON MERRILL

GREET THE UNSEEN
WITH A CHEER!

*"The greatest joy of joys shall be
the joy of going on"*

GREET THE UNSEEN
WITH A CHEER!

"Fare Ever There As Here"

No, at noonday in the bustle of man's worktime
   Greet the unseen with a cheer!
Bid him forward, breast and back as either should be,
"Strive and thrive!" cry, "Speed—fight on, fare ever
   There as here!"

ROBERT BROWNING

The Great Adventure

A minister and a noted chemist were walking in an academic procession. As the line halted momentarily, they noticed a lad of about thirteen. The minister asked the chemist how he would like to be the age of that boy in order to see the strides of chemical science during the next half-century. "No, I think not," was the surprising reply. Pressed for an explanation, the chemist told how his belief in evolution made personal immortality seem altogether reasonable. "Moreover," he continued, "I am a Christian man, and my faith extends beyond the border in the assurance that every honest longing of my soul for character, consciousness, and achievement shall find realization. Therefore, I watch the sands of life run low without regret. I am standing before the veil and waiting a summons. When it comes I shall greet it with a cheer. I am satisfied that this boy shall plod his way on the low level and see the unsuspected marvels yet unborn, while I strike the higher level in a world of pure spirit. I am just as eager to make that venture as I have joyfully lived my mortal career."

CORNELIUS WOLFKIN

Testimony from Antiquity

Approximately A.D. 125 a Greek by the name of Aristides was writing to one of his friends about the new religion, Christianity. He was trying to explain the reasons for its extraordinary success. Here is a sentence from one of his letters: "If any righteous man among the Christians passes from this world, they rejoice and offer thanks to God and they escort his body with songs and thanksgiving as if he were setting out from one place to another near by." What a description of Christian faith in immortality!

JOHN L. GEHMAN

Song in the Night

Ice breaks many a branch, and so I see a great many persons bowed down and crushed by their afflictions. But now and then I meet one that sings in affliction, and then I thank God for my own sake as well as his. There is no such sweet singing as a song in the night. You recollect the story of the woman who, when her only child died, in rapture looking up, as with the face of an angel, said, "I give you joy, my darling." That single sentence has gone with me years and years down through my life, quickening and comforting me.

HENRY WARD BEECHER

Death But Going on a Journey

If a dear friend is leaving us for a trip to Europe, we talk volubly about all he is to see, about art galleries and palaces and hotels and the quaint ways of foreign lands. But if a friend is about to go to heaven, we have nothing to say. Is it because there is, at bottom, a basic unbelief in what may lie beyond? Why are we so hesitant and so embarrassed? Do we really believe that beyond the bounds of this life our friends, departing, enter a life not less but more personal than the life lived here on earth?

If we believe that, why don't we talk that way? I want no conspiracy of silence in my own sick chamber.

If I cannot face the fact of near approaching death with level eyes and with untroubled heart and talk it over as calmly as I would discuss a trip to Europe, then all that I have preached to others is a lie.

There is much to be said for the unusual and somewhat eccentric habit of John Smith, Master of Harrow, one of England's great public schools. When he heard of one of his friends who was nearing death, he would rush in and warmly congratulate him. Why not? It seemed eccentric, but it was truly Christian.

M. H. Lichliter

A Poet Faces the Sunrise

The dean of modern American poets is no longer with us, but those of us who remember Edwin Markham think of him as always, even to his latest years, looking forward with eagerness. When he was past seventy-five he would greet his friends with the cheering words, "I am still facing the sunrise." At fourscore years he published his last volume entitled *Songs at Eighty*. One of his latest poems was entitled "The Look Ahead." Here it is:

"I am done with the years that were: I am quits:
    I am done with the dead and old.
They are mines worked out: I delved in their pits:
    I have saved their grain of gold.

"Now I turn to the future for wine and bread:
   I have bidden the past adieu.
I laugh and lift hand to the years ahead:
   Come on: I am ready for you!"

When Mr. Markham was asked to contribute to a volume of testimony on the subject of Immortality, he responded with these challenging words:

"Does man survive the grave? If he does we ought to know something about it, for that fact would have a great deal to do with our daily life. For it is a beautiful thing to look far ahead—to take the short step with a long look. I believe there are more revelations of the life to come. I believe that God is a divine dramatist; that he has created a great drama with many exits and many entrances; that this life is only one scene in this Romance of the Infinite.

"Now it looks as though the footsteps die out at the grave. We see no footsteps going beyond. But the wise know that seemings are often deceptive. We see the stars set; yet no star goes down but it climbs another sky. So I believe that when the soul disappears from one world, it disappears only to enter upon another scene in the wondrous Romance of Eternity. . . .

"Well, we are here. Some Power has called us out of the unknown. We did not come of our own wills. Some Higher Power has evolved it all. And the Power that has caused this revelation of wonder and mystery can easily have prepared for us another surprise beyond the locked mystery of death. And I believe that this stu-

pendous Power we call God has created another world,
a world of spirit for the spirit of man."

Toward the close of his remarkable career Edwin
Markham wrote a poem which puts into verse what he
testified earlier in prose. The poem is entitled "An Epi-
taph," and it reads:

"Let us not think of our departed dead
  As caught and cumbered in their graves of earth;
  But think of death as of another birth,
  As a new freedom for the wings outspread,
  A new adventure waiting on ahead,
  As a new joy of more ethereal mirth,
  As a new world with friends of nobler worth,
  Where all may taste a more immortal bread.

"So, comrades, if you pass my grave sometime,
  Pause long enough to breathe this little rhyme:
  'Here now the dust of Edwin Markham lies,
  But lo, he is not here: he is afar
  On life's great errands under mightier skies,
  And pressing on toward some melodious star.' "

THOMAS CURTIS CLARK

A Christian Sailor Embarks

Edward Shillito tells of the passing of a dear friend. This
man, head of a large business, an artist, a statesman, and
a loyal servant of Christ and the church, was preparing

to leave it all for his final voyage. He knew it. Everybody knew it. He set his house in order with deliberation. He asked for the newspapers each day and watched eagerly the trend of events. He made the most of his last days with his family, talking with them with no touch of morbid emotionalism. He dictated notes to friends in trouble and in joy. Then the end came. Mr. Shillito adds: "He knew that he was soon to go to his Lord; and with very good cheer he went, as one might wave farewell from the deck of a ship starting on its way."

M. H. LICHLITER

The Friendly Face of Death

"God forgive me if I am wrong," said Charles Kingsley of his approaching death, "but I look forward to it with an intense and reverent curiosity." So it seemed to Thomas Carlyle: "Eternity, which cannot be far off now, is my one strong city. I look into it fixedly now and then. All terrors about it seem superfluous." So it seemed to the old Christian who wrote the thrilling song of triumph with which the Bible ends. What a fair face it wore to him! What a friendly face! He calls it Christ, and it is the voice of Christ he records in style and language of his own:

"I am the Alpha and I the Omega,
   The beginning and also the ending,

The first one and likewise the last one.
And the spirit and the bride say, Come.
And the hearer, let him too say, Come.
And the thirsty, let him surely come.
Yea, whosoever will, let him come
And take of the water of life freely."

FRANK H. FERRIS

Traveling Hopefully

A strange picture we make on our way to our chimeras, ceaselessly marching, grudging ourselves the time for rest: indefatigable, adventurous pioneers.

It is true we shall never reach the goal; it is even more than probable that there is no such place; and if we lived for centuries and were endowed with the powers of a god we should find ourselves not much nearer what we wanted at the end. O toiling hands of mortals! O unwearied feet, traveling ye know not whither! Soon, soon, it seems to you, you must come forth on some conspicuous hill top, and but a little way further, against the setting sun, descry the spires of El Dorado. Little do ye know your own blessedness, for to travel hopefully is a better thing than to arrive, and the true success is to labor.

ROBERT LOUIS STEVENSON

"O.K., Lawd"

New York City was unusually moved by the death of Wesley Hill, who played the angel Gabriel in "The Green Pastures." Hill was run down by a taxicab while on his way home from a performance of that great Negro play. The most moving episode that has come out of this tragic close to a brilliant artistic career is contained in an episode reported by the newspapers. When Richard B. Harrison, who played the role of "De Lawd" in the play, and a group of the other actors visited the undertaker's parlors, he said, in words suggested by his part: "Now, Gabe, you look after things till we come." And the other actors, looking at the unmoving lips, made Gabriel's usual reply: "O.K., Lawd."

THE CHRISTIAN CENTURY

Trumpets for a Funeral

A soldier who participated in the invasion of North Africa was given a leave from his medical duties which permitted him to visit St. Augustine's church at Hippo. He described the beautiful altar and the crucifix completely surrounded by sandbags to protect this symbol from destruction. Indeed, with the figure of the dead Jesus upon a cross, we have a symbol of an event in antiquity the memory of which may remind us of suffering and death prompted by love.

But this is never an adequate interpretation of the Cross for the salvation of men. The true symbol of Christianity is the empty cross, and indeed the empty tomb. No two-dimensional view known to man is adequate to send men hopefully to die or even to suffer unto death for righteousness and truth. Yet, with the perspective which Jesus gives us through the Cross one may look forward to death as a fitting and logical climax to the Christian life on earth. At the funeral of Robert Browning in Westminster Abbey, Sir Edward Burne-Jones said: "I would have given something for a banner or two and much more I would have given if a chorister had come out and rent the air with a trumpet."

W. H. ROBERTS

A Triumphant Spirit

One of the most interesting soldiers in the British army during the First World War was Donald Hankey, a lieutenant in the Royal Warwickshire Regiment. He was an Oxford man, a lover of the poor, and of Christ. It was he who gave us the unforgettable sentence, "True religion is betting your life that there is a God." As the brave Hankey left England for his last campaign he wrote to a friend: "I feel singularly at ease. There is only one trag-edy in life, and that is the loss of God's love; and of that I feel too confident to be afraid. There is no other tragedy."

On the twelfth of October, 1916, orders came to go "over the top." At two o'clock, just before the zero hour, Hankey asked the men in his section of the trench if he might pray with them. After the prayer he spoke these heartening words: "Remember, men, if wounded, 'Blighty'; if killed, the resurrection." When he was last seen alive he was rallying his men, who had wavered under heavy machine-gun and rifle fire. He carried the waverers along with him, and was found that night close to the trench the winning of which cost him his life.

For him it was the resurrection! In the same confidence we can know that death will for us yield only life, richer, more adventurous, eternal—through the power of the risen Christ.

W. Taliaferro Thompson

"The Dream Is True!"

Life's significances, after all, are not in life's beginnings, but in life's endings. The fidelities that count are the fidelities that carry on and carry through. Edwin Mark-ham had in him the pith of the matter when he sang:

"Ah, great it is to believe the dream
    As we stand in youth by the starry stream,
    But a greater thing is to fight life through
    And say at the end, 'The dream is true.'"

                                    GEORGE H. COMBS

"With a Cheer"

John Rathbone Oliver told of a friend of his, a young physician, who met an untimely death. He was brilliant and assured of a distinguished future. He had married a young woman whom he had known from early youth. They seemed to be an ideal pair. Then came the end, after one year of married life. A chance infection from an autopsy, then the young woman was left a widow. Dr. Oliver confessed with shame that he did not go to the funeral. He who had written about how to overcome fear was afraid even to look at his bereaved friend. At last one morning he ran into her outside the hospital.

But this young woman wore no black. "Her face was alight with something more than mere happiness." The doctor mumbled some lame excuse for not having seen her in her time of sorrow. She patted his rather shaky hand. "Ah, Doctor, you don't understand," she said. "I miss Dick. Of course I miss him. But I haven't room in my heart for anything but thankfulness and gratitude to God. I had a year of Dick's love—a whole year of perfect happiness. No other woman has had as much as I. If I live to be eighty, I shall not have had time to thank God enough. And when I do stop living, well, Dick and I will be living together again."

G. RAY JORDAN

ETERNITY—HERE AND NOW

Today Partakes of Immortality

ETERNITY—HERE AND NOW

"To Each Man Is Given a Day"

To each man is given a day and his work for the day;
And once, and no more, he is given to travel this way.
And woe if he flies from the task, whatever the odds;
For the task is appointed to him on the scroll of the gods.

EDWIN MARKHAM

Building Immortality Here

St. Augustine said, with reference to that other land: "We do not go in ships or chariots or on horses or even on foot, but to go thither, nay, even to arrive, is nothing but to will to go." Actually we all live in two worlds, the physical and the spiritual, and constantly oscillate between the two. Every worthy aspiration, all love of truth or beauty, all earnest efforts after righteousness, every act of love and every true prayer, are so many excursions into that other world. If we are earnestly doing these things, then we are building up in this material body an inner spiritual structure adapted to that spiritual environment where it must continue to live; the grave can no more hold it than the grave could hold our Lord himself.

G. ASHTON OLDHAM

Living for Two Worlds

This story is told of the revered William R. Wedderspoon, for many years a Chicago pastor. It is the story of a conversation Dr. Wedderspoon had with a business man of Chicago. The minister had conducted the funeral service of another business man. In the course of his funeral discourse Dr. Wedderspoon had said simply: "My brothers, we are living for two worlds." After the service was over, this business friend of the deceased man came forward and challenged the statement. "Why, you believe that, don't you?" the minister asked. "No, sir," instantly replied the business man, "I do not. And what is more, most of the men here today did not believe it either." The good minister was astounded. "You do not believe that we are living for two worlds?" he again asked. "No, sir," came the quick response; "we are living for one world and one only. We do not know of any other world than this. We shape our lives this way, and our business too." The minister was silent for a moment, then he asked: "If you did believe in another world than this, would it make any difference to you?" The reply came without hesitation: "Of course it would. If I had the slightest suspicion that we are living for any other world than this, I would change every major business policy I have before night!"

W. Howard Lee

Life Begins—Now!

Do you think you are alive enough to rise from the dead? How long do you suppose you will have to wait to settle that question? If I were you, I'd settle it right now. "Life begins at—," just your age, if it hasn't begun for you before. And will that question stay settled? No, it will not. You will have to keep at it every day, growing your rings—living your life at its fullest and best.

> "Build thee more stately mansions, O my soul,
>   As the swift seasons roll!
>   Leave thy low-vaulted past!
>   Let each new temple, nobler than the last,
>   Shut thee from heaven with a dome more vast,
>   Till thou at length art free,
>   Leaving thine outgrown shell by life's unresting
>   sea!"

Willard B. Thorp

Eternity Around Us

The story is told of certain sailors who were near death with thirst. Ocean water being worse than no water at all, they were like the Ancient Mariner who moaned, "Water, water everywhere, but not a drop to drink." Soon they met a boat and, overjoyed, asked the sailors for a drink of fresh water. Their new companions, surprised at their request, told them to lower their buckets and help themselves. The mariners had thought that they were in the open ocean. As a matter of fact they were at least a mile up the Amazon river. Eternal life is often conceived as something far off. Jesus thought of it as something which we may taste here and now. Its resources are all around us, not on some distant shore.

CARL KNUDSEN

Immortality from Within

"Immortality is not some destiny conferred from without," says R. H. Murray, "but the flower of fruitage which must be developed from within." Again he declares: "It is not like the gift of knighthood as when a man kneels before a royal sovereign a plebeian, and at the touch of a sword rises an aristocrat, a titled gentleman. It is the life of Christ in the soul, blushing with imperishable youth." Richter had the same idea when he said: "We desire immortality, not as a reward of virtue, but as its continuance."

We Are in Eternity

Nowhere in the Gospels can we find Jesus talking about immortality. He talked about "eternal life." Immortality is merely a going on and on. Eternal life is life so rich and significant that it makes going on and on desirable. Immortality is post-mortem; eternal life is now. We cannot prepare for eternity, for thinking in the terms of eternal life we are now in eternity. As Richard Jeffries wrote: "The question is not, 'Where will you spend eternity?' but 'Where are you spending it?'" If we hope to go on advancing, unfolding, growing, developing after death, we must be participating now in eternal life.

Richard Jeffries also said: "It is eternity now. I am in the midst of it. It is about me in the sunshine; I am in it as the butterfly floats in the sun-laden air." Eternal life is, indeed, all about us, waiting to be lived. It is a quality of life in the present, received from Christ and serving ends that his spirit would approve and bless.

H. RICHARD RASMUSSON

Life That Is Life Indeed

It is not because this present life is dull or burdensome or unfruitful that our hearts so often meditate upon the heavenly life, but because that life is so truly a part of ourselves. We are creatures of two worlds, and while we find inspirations and satisfactions here, we know that we are made for even fuller and richer life than this world affords. Therefore, in the midst of our most zestful activities there steal into our hearts hints and dreams of the life that is life indeed.

HERBERT L. WILLETT

A Present Possession

The New Testament is not concerned about an endless existence, but about eternal life. Most men would refuse to entertain the idea that this life is to continue endlessly. Many would refuse to accept the continuous existence of today's kind of life. They desire something better. The Christian faith declares that believers in Jesus Christ will have eternal life in the kingdom of God where they are to share the life of God. And that eternal life begins here and now—a present possession, not a future reward.

RALPH C. MCAFEE

"The Hint of Eternity"

Lorado Taft, the American sculptor, whose fine work may be seen in some of our great cities, was speaking to a friend about his own art and about those who worked with him in the same line. He said to a friend: "What we sculptors need is to get back into our work the hint of eternity." There is a good deal of deep significance in that word, not for sculptors alone, but for other artists and workers as well. What our painters need is to get some farther and deeper meaning into their canvases. What our composers need is to get away from jazz and get some accent of eternity in their compositions, to make them comparable to the work of the great masters. Indeed all of us, whatever our work or art, need that accent, that subtle emphasis, which reveals the deep conviction that we belong essentially in the eternal order.

ALFRED W. WISHART

Fitting Oneself for Heaven

It is said that when a student in a moral philosophy class of Mark Hopkins once asked him who would go to heaven, Hopkins replied that he did not know but that he was sure no one would be there who did not feel at home.

MARGUERITTE H. BRO

Build Immortality Now!

The one thing which otherwise careful and intelligent people neglect more than any other is the future of their immortal souls. You have within you an immortal part not to be touched or changed by death. What are you doing to assure the future of your soul? The future of that soul is being built today. What its destiny will be rests within the power of your own two hands. Do not be careless about this. It is your greatest opportunity. Build now, through reverence and charity and honesty and prayer, a future for your immortal soul! A poet has said most eloquently all that I have been saying:

> "Let me make spacious plans,
>   Not such as can be bound
>   By years, but caravans
>   Of hope, whose songs resound
>   Across the unknown spans
>   Of Heaven's gracious ground,
>   Where pioneering man's
>   Eternal home is found!"
>
> WILLIAM R. MOODY

The Way to God

Did you say you cannot think of God because your mind has no satisfying concept? You have no image of Life, but you have it, and you know it. The life more abundant and richer in quality—that is God. When its wealth flowers in love, you are in God, and God is in you. Life Eternal is God. God is Life Eternal. It, or he, is flowing through you now. Let it flow more freely, more purely, and the river is entering the Sea. "This life" manifestly takes on the qualities of Life Eternal.

FREDERICK W. NORWOOD

The Best Proof

The best proof of immortality, after all, rests not so much in demonstrating the continuance of life as in sharing here and now the life of God.

CHARLES F. WISHART

What Is Immortality?

Immortality is not something to be improvised at death. Rather it is the slow accumulation of the years. It is the product of a life lived after the pattern of Jesus Christ.

HAROLD L. LUNGER

Reaching the Mountain Top

Akaba was the captain of a robber band. His treasuries were filled with the countless stores which he had stolen. His mind, however, was ill at ease. He came to Ben-Achmet, a dervish, renowned for his sanctity, living on the borders of a wilderness in Arabia, and thus addressed him: "Five hundred swords obey my nod, innumerable slaves bow to my control, my storehouses are filled with silver and gold; tell me, how can I add to all these the hope of eternal life?"

The dervish led him to a rugged mountain track,

pointed to three immense stones, bade him take them and follow him to the top of the hill. "My son," said the hermit when they sat on the top, "you have a threefold burden to hinder you on the road to a better state. Dismiss the robber band, set the slaves free, give back your ill-gotten gain. Sooner would Akaba reach the mountain top bearing those heavy stones than find real happiness in power, lust, and wealth." Akaba obeyed the hermit.

R. W. Everroad

John Wesley on Death

When asked what he would do if he knew that he would die on a particular night, John Wesley replied that he would partake of his evening meal, preach at candlelight, say his prayers, and retire in sleep as usual—which is to say that in the face of death he would adhere to his established routine of life.

Anonymous

Eternity—Now

We are not preparing for eternity now, we are even now in eternity. And whatever takes place after the body dies, it will be for the participant in eternal life the continuance of that Christian joy and service begun here and

now. "This *is* life eternal, to know Thee." In the words
of John Masefield we seek:

> "A light that darkness cannot smirch, a peace
>   That torment cannot break, a Life that Death
>   Is powerless to kill, being life eternal."
>
> H. RICHARD RASMUSSON

The Best Preparation

Many a life has been injured by the constant expectation
of death. It is life we have to do with, not death. The
best preparation for the night is to work diligently while
the day lasts. The best preparation for death is life.

GEORGE MACDONALD

The Cost of Immortality

Dr. Cornelius Woelfkin, in his book *Expanding Hori-
zons*, tells of a conversation he had with a biologist as
they were seated one day on a bench at a golf course.
When Dr. Woelfkin asked the scientist whether biology
had discovered anything to confirm faith in immortality,
the biologist replied in the negative, but added this significant remark: "I have a feeling that until a man
espouses either a cause or an individual for which he is

perfectly willing to jeopardize his life and would count it an honor to die, he does not come within sight of immortality."

ALBERT J. BUTZER

Getting Fit to Live

You recall William James' reply to the query: "Do you believe in a personal immortality?" "Never keenly; but more strongly as I grow older." "Why?" "Because I am just getting fit to live."

RALPH W. SOCKMAN

In an Eternal Universe

The man who lives as though he were immortal lives in a universe where the highest spiritual values are permanent, outlasting the growth and dissolution of the stars; where character is the supreme concern of life. We are not digging artificial lakes to be filled by our own buckets, in hopeless contest with an alien universe, but are rather building channels down which the eternal spiritual purpose of the living God shall flow to its "far-off divine event." The truth of immortality makes great living.

HARRY EMERSON FOSDICK

Life All of a Piece

Here is the great discovery that awaits us: life is all of a piece. "We are not someday going to be, we already are immortal spirits."

MAUDE ROYDEN

Now—and Then

I delight in the feeling that I am in eternity, that I can serve God now fully and effectively, that the next piece of road will come in sight when I am ready to walk in it.

FORBES ROBINSON

Preparing Now for Eternal Life

The more we are raised above the petty vexations and pleasures of this world into the eternal life to come, the more shall we be prepared to enter into that eternal life whenever God shall please to call us hence.

ARTHUR P. STANLEY

FAITH THAT LOOKS
THROUGH DEATH

The "Solid Certainty" Brought by Christ

FAITH THAT LOOKS
THROUGH DEATH

"We Will Grieve Not"

We will grieve not, rather find
Strength in what remains behind;
In the primal sympathy
Which having been must ever be;
In the soothing thoughts that spring
Out of human suffering;
In the faith that looks through death,
In years that bring the philosophic mind.

WILLIAM WORDSWORTH

It Doth Not Yet Appear

How and where this immortal life goes on, I do not
know, and am more and more content not to ask. "It
doth not yet appear what we shall be." Our thought of

life under other conditions than these, like our thought of God, must inevitably be in pictures drawn from the life that now is. But I find that it always matters much less where one is, than whom one is with. That familiar fact gives its own intimate comfort and thrilling hope to the assurance of Christian faith, that those whom we have loved and lost a while are "together with Christ," in the presence where there is fullness of joy and the fountain of life itself.

CHARLES W. GILKEY

"If It Were Not So—"

An ultimate argument for immortality is the instinctive intuition of the human soul. There was a profound truth in the mind of Browning when he built for Abt Vogler a Temple of Melody up which the organist made his way to a height whence he could look out on life from above and see it as the angels see it. There he observed that the broken arcs ultimately become round; that the broken aspirations of man are completed; that man's noblest dreams are realized. And then the organist was led back to earth with this substantial philosophy: "God has a few of us to whom he whispers in the ear; the rest may reason, but 'tis we musicians who know." There is genuine insight.

Once, twice, perhaps thrice in a life under some stress of sorrow, straining our ears we hear a reassuring voice, and shading our eyes we see intimations of an immortality to be. The Christian heart believes that if these intimations and instincts were not so, Jesus would have told us. We rest our faith in immortality upon the reliability of Jesus. He knew our longings and understood our intuitions. Had there been no objective reality in the direction in which they point, he would have told us. On the contrary, while he did not explain the after life, he gave us sublime hope by assuring us that our intuitions are trustworthy—"If it were not so, I would have told you."

NORMAN VINCENT PEALE

Proofs of Immortality

What is our proof of immortality? Not the analogies of nature—the resurrection of nature from a winter grave— or the emancipation of the butterfly. Not even the testimony to the fact of risen dead; for who does not know how shadowy and unsubstantial these intellectual proofs become in unspiritual frames of mind? No; the life of the spirit is the evidence. Heaven begun is the living proof that makes the heaven to come credible. "Christ in you is the hope of glory." It is the eagle eye of faith which penetrates the grave, and sees far into the tranquil things of death. He alone can believe in immortality who feels the resurrection in him already.

FREDERICK W. ROBERTSON

We Do Not Believe in Death

As followers of Christ, in whom the very heart of God has been unveiled, we do not believe in death. Even as thousands fall at our left and ten thousands at our right, we still do not believe in death. For we Christians know that the breath of eternal life is in us. So we are undaunted by the holocausts of time. We are channels of God's breath of life made known to us in Christ.

RUSSELL H. STAFFORD

Not an Achievement of Reasoning

"Now are we the sons of God, and it doth not yet appear what we shall be; but we know that when he shall be manifested we shall be like him." The faith in a future life of the early Christians was not an achievement of reasoning, but a consciousness of the presence of Christ who could not be holden of death. There are some good philosophical arguments for immortality, but the best of them are hard to grasp and frail to lean upon. However, the Christian faith in eternal life does not rest upon these arguments. It rests at last upon the character of God. His character was revealed in Jesus Christ who vanquished death and brought immortality to light. Such a God will not cast his children to the void. The earnest of man's immortality is his possession of eternal life now—that new

life which the living presence of Christ bestows upon all
who love and obey him.

CHARLES CLAYTON MORRISON

Two Fundamental Questions

The fundamental questions about immortality are two:
Is it desirable? and, Is it believable? Dante suggests the
way to an affirmative answer to both questions when he
describes a procession of the virtues in which Hope never
leads but always follows, sometimes after Love and sometimes after Faith. The hope of immortality is motivated
by human love, and it gains certitude from faith in the
reality and sufficiency of God. The way to reassurance
of God and immortality is not primarily the way of argument and coercive proof, but rather that of cultivating
the soil out of which these convictions normally grow.

DOUGLAS C. MACINTOSH

Death an Incident

I must live after this life because God lives. He has been
building up in me a part of himself. These values may
change but they cannot cease to be. Death is an incident
in their growth and adjustment. The spiritual aspirations
of all ages stand up as witnesses that cannot be brow-

beaten. This life is transitory; the other life must be permanent to satisfy both God and ourselves.

PETER AINSLIE

Phillips Brooks Writes a Letter

The following letter, written to a grieving husband, was found in Phillips Brooks' own handwriting in a volume of his sermons:

My dear Friend: I have thought much about our meeting last Sunday, and the words we had together. May I try to tell you again where your only comfort lies? It is not in forgetting the happy past. People bring us well-meant but miserable consolation when they tell us what *time* will do to help our grief. We do not want to lose our grief, because our grief is bound up with our love and we could not cease to mourn without being robbed of our affection. But if you know—as you do know—that the great and awful change which has come into your life and brought you such distress has brought your dear wife the joy of heaven, can you not, in the midst of all your suffering, rejoice for her? And if, knowing she is with God, you can be with God too, and every day claim his protection and try to do his will, may you not still in spirit be very near to her?

She is not dead, but living, and if you are sure what care is holding her, and educating her, you can be very contentedly with her in spirit and look forward confidently to the day when you shall also go to God and be with her. I know this does not take away your pain— no one can do that—you do not want anyone to do that —not even God; but it can help you to bear it, to be brave and cheerful, to do your duty, and to live the pure, earnest, spiritual life which she, in heaven, wishes you to live. It is the last effort of unselfishness, the last token which you can give her of the love you bear her, that you can let her pass out of your sight to go to God. My dear friend, she is yours forever. God never takes away what he has once given. May he make you worthy of her! May he comfort you and make you strong.

Your friend, sincerely,

PHILLIPS BROOKS

In His Light We See Light

"Thanks be to God, who giveth us the victory through our Lord Jesus Christ." It is not only religious faith, it is deep and true rationality, it is high common sense, to take the view of Jesus. With what assurance he said to the sufferer at his side, "This day shalt thou be with me in Paradise." What quiet trust breathes in his last words: "Father, into thy hands I commend my spirit."

In his light we see light. Here, as everywhere, the deepest convictions of our hearts find confirmation in Christ. We know that God did not make man capable of growth, of desire, of nobility, of love, of passionate devotion, of loyalty to honor, of faith in God, only to be frustrated and forever unsatisfied. It is not grasping at a sentimental comfort, it is not the taking of an opiate; it is the calm exercise of our highest and best intelligence, the taking of the path of truest, surest wisdom, when we hear our Lord say: "Let not your heart be troubled; believe in God, believe also in me. In my Father's house are many mansions. I go to prepare a place for you"; and, in quiet trust and sure faith, look forward with confidence to the end of this chapter of our story; knowing well that as Phillips Brooks once said, death is like turning over a page in a book by an author we have learned to love and trust.

"We do not know what we shall find, but we know that it will be good." "No man hath seen God at any time." But, "I hope to see my Pilot face to face, when I have crossed the bar"; and "I shall be satisfied, when I awake, with his likeness."

WILLIAM PIERSON MERRILL

Christ Is God's Answer

As we meet the deep sorrows of life, as we stand beside the new-made grave, we need something more than speculations of philosophy or the guesses of human reason. The help that we need is given to us in Christ, the Son of God. It is Christ who has changed hope into assurance, speculation into faith, longing into certainty. In the risen Christ we have God's own answer to the longing which he has implanted in our souls.

WILLIAM T. MANNING

Trust in God's Goodness

Uncountable are the questions concerning life, death, the future life that we cannot answer. They are mysteries which the most scholarly can never penetrate. Yet all that matters little if only we have confidence in the unceasing goodness and kindness of God; enough to nourish within us the calm consciousness that we are in his hands and all is well; enough to inspire strength and peace. Warren Seabury, an American missionary in China, wrote: "I do not know what is before me, but I am building my nest in the greatness of God." That is the language and experience of the tranquil, trusting heart.

JOHNSTONE G. PATRICK

The Ground of Faith

Nobody else has anything to tell me about my future life. Christ has; with calm assurance he declares that he has. He knows, and he knows that he knows. What, then, does he tell me? He says: "Because I live, ye shall live also. In my father's palace are many apartments. If it were not so, I would have told you. I go to prepare a place for you. I am the resurrection and the life. Whosoever has seen me has seen the Father. This day shalt thou be with me in Paradise." There it is, plain and simple and clear. Like Emerson, Christ does not undertake to prove. He never undertook to prove God, but talked as if to little children about "my father and your father." So about endless life, he says in that simple, matter-of-fact fashion of his: "If it were not so, I would have told you." These words of his, this calm assumption, this placid certitude is the ground of my faith in unending life.

BURRIS JENKINS

A Solid Certainty

Christ turned a brilliant guess into a solid certainty and endowed the hope of eternal life with grace, reason, and majesty.

HUGH ELMER BROWN

The Testimony of Jesus

Jesus, and the New Testament, do not labor to prove that man lives after death. Life after death is a triumphant assertion of the Master and the writers of the New Testament; it is not the subject for weighty, exhaustive debate. Jesus proclaims a truth, he does not debate a hypothesis. Few persons are impressed or helped by arduous argument intended to prove that individuals survive physical death. William James, in his lectures on Immortality, declared that traditional arguments carry forward very little, if any, a person's belief in the triumph of life over death. We may well be grateful, therefore, that the authors of the New Testament start with an assertion, and that the creeds of Christendom end with what is a dramatic and logical conclusion based on the prior faith in God that has been affirmed: "*and* I believe in everlasting life."

CHARLES W. KEGLEY

The Assurance of Faith

When one of our own dies—a father or mother, a husband or wife, a son or daughter—one whom we love better than our own life—there is the real test. That we all might have the faith of William E. Barton which he voiced on the death of his beloved wife: "Now there will come a day when I also shall ascend the stair that slopeth upward from this mortal world to that which is above. And I know that she will be listening for my coming. Yea, and she will not altogether wait for me outside the gate: for I shall hear her footstep coming a little way down to meet me, and we shall go in together."

W. TALIAFERRO THOMPSON

Rooted in Eternity

How irrepressible is our soul's faith in its immortality! No plans for this life alone seem to satisfy us. All our satisfactions are rooted in eternity. God has not given us merely a logical proof, a scientific demonstration, of immortality, but he has organized immortality into the very structure of our soul. We are made for the Beyond as well as for the Here, and all skeptical thinking that casts doubt upon the soul's survival of death ignores the deep foundations of our nature.

HERBERT L. WILLETT

"I Shall Be Satisfied"

Tell me, apostle of unbelief, if you will, that I can frame no idea of future living that does not break down into absurdity. Call me selfish, egotistical, childish, to desire life beyond the grave. I will answer, Very well; have it so. But one thing I have a right to demand; and I have faith to believe that it will be granted: "I shall be satisfied, when I awake." God has made me to know something, to grow, to wonder, to question. Yes, and he has made me so that I count it worth while to defend my honor, to live for ideals, to fight for faith, to suffer if necessary for the right. He has made me to rejoice in love, and goodness, and loyalty, and all the great unseen values. And what I ask of him, what I have a right to assume that he will give me, is some final satisfaction that this higher life is not just a delusion. I want to know that the values of life are real. And if death ends all, then they are not real. Somehow God must satisfy my higher self, or he is not worthy of my attention or respect.

It is this conviction that keeps men believing, in the face of the terrible testimonies of the senses, in the face of the awful silence of the unseen, believing in life to come. We cannot believe that God would stultify himself. If there is any God worth taking into account, he will not leave so glorious a reality as the human spirit on an ash heap. We might consent to let our little lives sink into nothingness; God cannot afford to let the life he has made come to such an end.

WILLIAM PIERSON MERRILL

When Death Reveals God

Death is not always a matter of destruction; it sometimes creates in those who are bereaved something precious and eternal. Young Calvin Coolidge, Jr., died in Washington at the dawn of what promised to be an abundant and fruitful life. A year after his passing, Mrs. Coolidge wrote in her Northampton home:

> "You, my son,
>   Have shown me God.
>   Your kiss upon my cheek

Has made me feel the gentle touch
Of him who leads us on.
The memory of your smile, when young,
Reveals his face,
As mellowing years come on apace.
And when you went before,
You left the gates of Heaven ajar
That I might glimpse,
Approaching from afar,
The glories of his grace.
Hold, son, my hand,
Guide me along the path,
That, coming,
I may stumble not
Nor roam,
Nor fail to show the way
Which leads us—Home."

A Creed That Brings Delight

Life appears to me to be too short to be spent in nursing
animosities or in registering wrongs. We are, and must
be, one and all, burdened with faults in this world; but
the time will come when, I trust, we shall put them off in
putting off our corruptible bodies: when debasement and
sin will fall from us and only the spark will remain, the
impalpable principle of life and thought, pure as when
it left the Creator to inspire the creature: whence it

came, it will return, perhaps to pass through gradations of glory.

It is a creed in which I delight, to which I cling. It makes Eternity a rest, a mighty home; not a terror and an abyss. Besides, with this creed revenge never worries my heart, degradation never too deeply disgusts me, injustice never crushes me too low: I live in calm looking to the end.

GEORGE GISSING

Two Views of Life

There are two ways of looking at life. One is the way of sentiment; the other is the way of faith. The sentimental way is trite enough. Saint, sage, sophist, moralist, and preacher have repeated in every possible image, till there is nothing new to say, that life is a bubble, a dream, a delusion, a phantasm. The other is the way of faith. The ancient saints felt as keenly as any moralist could feel the brokenness of life's promises; they confessed that they were strangers and pilgrims here; they said that they had here no continuing city; but they did not mournfully moralize on this; they said it cheerfully, and rejoiced that it was so. They felt that all was right; they knew that the promise itself had a deeper meaning; they looked undauntedly for "a city which hath foundations."

FREDERICK W. ROBERTSON

The Anchor of Hope

Hope is not easily extinguished. It has a way of renewing itself. It sometimes even becomes stronger and more radiant under discouragement and long delay. It has power to hold on and to endure and to wait. More than that—it brings its own assurance of things not seen. It is a true word that tells us that there are those whose spirits have the power to see that which is invisible. The heart of the Christian hopes through and beyond even the valley of the shadow and believes, sometimes in spite of appearances and in spite of itself, in the better life that is to be.

J. PERCIVAL HUGET

Not a Demonstration

Only you can prove immortality to yourself, for it is not a demonstration nor a proposition. It is, and must ever be, a deep conviction or instinct. "The faith of immortality," says Horace Bushnell, "depends upon a sense of it begotten and not an argument for it concluded." James Martineau, with penetrative insight, declares: "We do not believe in immortality because we can prove it, but we try to prove it because we cannot help believing it."

NORMAN VINCENT PEALE

Christ Brought Immortality to Light

I believe in a future life because Jesus believed in it. Suppose for the sake of argument that he is not the Son of God in that unique sense which enables him to speak about religion as one having authority of firsthand knowledge! Suppose he has merely given us his opinion! Whose opinion on religious questions would I rather trust than his?

Moreover, he was able to certify to the consciousness of his contemporaries the fact that he was still alive after they had seen him die in a public place called Calvary. However it came about, Jesus Christ was more of a power in the streets of Jerusalem forty days after his death than he had been before. "He showed himself alive." That was the brief, forceful account given by his disciples. I hold with them that by his personal victory over death he brought immortality to light.

CHARLES R. BROWN

One World at a Time?

Christian faith must begin with the truth of the life everlasting. There are some persons who say they can wait. One world at a time is sufficient for them. But can they wait without concern, without despair? Does it make no difference for all the remainder of our life on earth whether by faith we accept Jesus' teaching that life is everlasting or consider that after a few brief years death is the end? Eternity in the heart of the writer of Ecclesiastes was a disappointment because he was not sure of an answering eternity in the providence of God. Can you keep eternity in your heart unless life is indeed immortal?

HAMPTON ADAMS

The Bravest Gesture of Humanity

Immortality is the bravest gesture of our humanity toward the unknown. It is always a faith, never a demonstration. It can be defended by argument, it is supported by authority, but I do not believe its hold upon us to depend either upon argument or authority. It is an aspect of our passion for life, the protest of personality that it is too valuable to be annihilated and especially since it has been realized through such stupendous processes. It gives to life a value death cannot destroy. Without it life would be a puzzled pilgrimage in the dark.

GAIUS GLENN ATKINS

My Son Liveth!

My son has passed on as he did everything else, bravely and courageously. From the depths of our sorrow, I would ask you to look past grief into a sustaining, won-

derfully comforting thought; for he has not passed into
death but into Life, and when we have somewhat recov-
ered from this time of shock and heartache, we shall realize that his life cannot be lost.

He was always a good boy, faithful to his convictions,
a seeker after truth, and unflagging in his quest of ways
to be of service. Think now of the force and influence
of that character and understanding in the next realm of
life into which he has passed.

We do not know a great deal about that next life, but
we can be pretty sure, from all that we know of this
one, that it is a life of progress, of growth and service.
Have you ever thought about what must, in these troubled times, be happening in that realm? Thousands of
lives thrust suddenly into the beyond! Not only young
men like him, but older men and women too, and little
children. Surely they must need help in becoming ad-
justed to that new life. Someone like John could help.
He would want to be where he could help the most.

Many will say that he was called before his time, but
we can be sure that he has been called to a Higher Service. He has been released to his new task, and although
seemingly lost to us, he has been promoted to a field of
service so wide and vast that perhaps none of us can as
yet begin to imagine its grandeur.

He has laid aside the familiar garment of the flesh—
it never seemed so strong as the spirit of him—to be
clothed anew in the shining raiment of those who love
and laugh and serve the Highest.

I have always been proud of him, and as I now see him find a new place of service, I feel a new pride and a deep sense of the "peace that passeth understanding."

HIS MOTHER

A New Order of Life

The important thing in Christ's revelation of immortality is not the fact that life goes on after death. Mere "going on" might not be very desirable—to some it would be terrible to go on forever the same poor old self. What Christ does is to announce and demonstrate a new kind of life, a new order of life which is essentially "eternal life." . . . To be "born of God" is to rise above the world and to live by forces and energies that are from beyond its spheres and limits.

RUFUS M. JONES

A Triumphant Challenge

For those who have had no deep experiences, whose religion is a thing of codes and rules, of gifts and rewards, whose thinking is concerned with material things, to speak of a resurrection is an irrelevance, for there is nothing to survive. But those whose eyes are opened to behold things invisible, whose thoughts dwell on things above—seekers after truth and goodness who during their earthly pilgrimage have constructed that building not made with hands—well may shout with St. Paul his triumphant challenge to the powers of darkness: "O death, where is thy sting? O grave, where is thy victory?"

G. ASHTON OLDHAM

Immortality Widens Horizons

A man without a belief in the future is like a man who does not breathe more than an inch in his lungs; he is short of breath, as it were, like a man with the consumption: but the moment he believes in endless existence he is like a man who breathes freely and fully. A man who has no belief in immortality is like a man in a prison; but a man who believes that ere long the stroke of death which shatters him will shatter the material elements by which he is confined in this life, and make his horizon boundless—how large a manhood there is in him! What a refuge to him is the thought of the everlasting!

PHILLIPS BROOKS

Going Home in the Dark

When O. Henry, the famous storyteller, lay dying, he called to his nurse: "Nurse, light me a candle if you please; I am afraid to go home in the dark." Had he

known the Living Light he would not have known fear
but trust; he would have been content to place himself
completely in the Master's keeping, singing in his heart
these words of Cardinal Newman's faith:

> "So long Thy power has blest me, sure it still
>   Will lead me on;
> O'er moor and fen, o'er crag and torrent, till
>   The night is gone.
> And with the morn those angel faces smile,
> Which I have loved long since and lost awhile."
>
> ANONYMOUS

Joy Comes Tomorrow

Today's tears will be followed by tomorrow's smiles.
"Weeping may endure for a night, but joy cometh in the
morning." In this, our Father's world, planned and ruled
by him, we may be educated by suffering, winnowed out
by tribulation; but the joyous reward is as sure as the
stability of God. Our generation writes Today in capital
letters; Eternal Wisdom capitalizes the long Tomorrow.
Sometimes faith endures today for the sake of tomorrow. All the plans of God, to whom a thousand years are
as a day, are long plans. And we shall have the limitless
length of eternity to understand and enjoy them.

WILLIAM T. ELLIS

Eternity Glimpsed Through Christ

To his first disciples the attraction of Jesus lay not in some special gift of personal magnetism with which he was endowed, but in a kind of atmosphere of eternity of which his presence always made his friends aware. The heart craves to be lifted above the sensuous and petty and finite into the ideal and spiritual sphere. Jesus satisfied this craving in his disciples. He seemed to them to bring the ancient years into the present moment, and to carry the present moment into the boundless future, thus touching their finite lives with the infinite and the eternal.

HERBERT L. WILLETT

The Goodness of God

Everything is grounded on the character of God, on his goodness, his faithfulness, his fatherliness. It would be a denial of God's own nature if his children could be overcome by death.

To enter into fellowship with God is to enter a relationship that death cannot enter. He to whom God has given his friendship is one with him forever. A God who at the last could leave men in the grave would not be the God whom Jesus knew. "Would it not be blasphemy," wrote Wordsworth in his bereavement, "to say we have more of love in our nature than he has? The thought is monstrous; and yet how to get rid of it except upon the supposition of another and a better world, I do not see."

ROBERT J. McCRACKEN

"Here Is the Road"

"Where is Kandersteg?" a traveler in Switzerland asked a lad one day when they met on the road. "I do not know," said the boy, "but there's the road that leads to it." Neither do we know just where the land of our hopes is, but some of us happily and boldly assert: "Here is the road—Jesus Christ!"

G. RAY JORDAN

Death—and a Song

John Oxenham, the British poet, was asked by a friend how he came to write one of his most beautiful poems. The poet then told how he had received from the war department a message concerning his son, who had been in the midst of some fierce fighting. The message read: "Killed in action." Hardly knowing what to do, the stricken father went to a little London chapel. In the semidarkness he sat, bewildered; but at last a great peace came into his soul, and he wrote the poem containing these lines:

" 'Mid all the traffic of the ways,
  Turmoils without, within,
Make in my heart a quiet place
  And come and dwell therein;

"A little shrine of quietness,
  All sacred to thyself,
Where thou shalt all my soul possess—
  And I may find myself."

God, the Soul, Immortality

There are three facts which have been fundamental in life, three ideas which have haunted man and would not let him go; with which he has had to wrestle until the breaking of the day. These three are God, the Soul, and Immortality. Man has tried to grasp them up and unify them and see them under one principle. Christianity has taught him how. It has given him an infinite Father, the essence of whose life is love; it has given him an infinite soul, a soul boundless in its aspirations and desires; and it has given him an infinite time in which to work out the problems of his life. These are the three things which have always been haunting man and they are all infinite, they are all eternal, and they belong together. They show man, as he has never been shown before, that he has time to build his life in a splendid and enduring way.

FREDERIC E. DEWHURST

Only a Step

Jesus gave us the thought of eternal life. Amid the threatening clouds of death, he consoles his disciples; only "a little while and ye shall see me. I go to the Father." Here opens an entirely new world. The ancients had spoken of Hades, but they trembled at the thought of it. The Jews had some nebulous notion of the beyond. But here was calm assurance. Only a step from time to eternity! It is merely the return to the Father from whom we came. What an abundance of thought and inspiration has sprung from this belief! It has sustained martyrs, made heroes, strengthened faith.

"What is our failure here but a triumph's evidence
For the fullness of days?"

ANDREAS BARD

A New Continent

Death is a great adventure, but none need go unconvinced that there is an issue in it. The man of faith may face it as Columbus faced his first voyage from the shores of Spain. What lies across the sea, he cannot tell; his special expectations all may be mistaken; but his insight into the clear meanings of present facts may persuade him beyond doubt that the sea has another shore. Such confident faith, so founded upon reasonable grounds, shall be turned to sight when, for all the disbelief of the unbelieving, the hope of the seers is rewarded by the vision of a new continent.

HARRY EMERSON FOSDICK

EASTER HORIZONS

Resurrection Is Written
All Over Christianity

EASTER HORIZONS

"Heaven with Its New Day"

Easter day breaks!
Christ rises! Mercy every way is infinite—
Earth breaks up; time drops away;
In flows heaven with its new day
Of endless life. . .

ROBERT BROWNING

Dawn!

One of the most thrilling experiences I ever had was
from a mountain top—Mt. St. Thomas in the Philippine
Islands. A little party of us started early one morning
to climb the mountain. All that day we climbed toward
the beckoning goal, pausing now and then from sheer
exhaustion. Up, ever up, until at sunset we reached the

top. That night, wrapped in heavy blankets, we slept in a little bunkhouse on the top of the mountain. We were up early the next morning, while it was yet dark, to see the sun rise. I remember standing on a height that dropped precipitously—the tops of tall pines at our feet. We looked to the east, over the vast Pacific. We caught the first glimmerings of the day. Then dawn, dawn: "Out of darkness the world rolled into light. Daybreak, daybreak everywhere!"

Easter brings us to the mountain top. We are on a privileged height, waiting for the sun to rise upon an expectant world. How better can we say what is in our hearts than by the use of Matthew's morning word— Dawn!

BRUCE S. WRIGHT

The Message of Easter

The Easter assurance changes faith. It takes the panic from our hearts and sets us in harmony with a mighty plan that leads to a noble destiny. More than this, it revolutionizes daily conduct. To grasp the meaning of life that lies beyond our earthly passions, gives dignity to life's task and to the soul of every comrade on the earth. Cynicism, superficial pursuits go when we grasp the moral dignity of human existence which is lived in view of Eternal Reality.

ROBERT MERRILL BARTLETT

"Christ Is Alive!"

The late Dr. Dale was writing an Easter sermon, and when halfway through, the thought of the risen Lord broke in upon him as it had never done before.

" 'Christ is alive,' I said to myself: 'alive!' and then I paused—'alive! Can that really be true—living as really as I am?' I got up and walked about repeating, 'Christ is living! Christ is living!' At first it seemed strange and hardly true, but at last it came upon me as a burst of sudden glory; yes, Christ lives! It was to me a new discovery. I thought that all along I had believed it; but not until that moment did I feel sure about it. I then said: 'My people shall know it; I shall preach about it again and again until they believe it as I do now.' "

For months afterward, and in every sermon, the Living Christ was Dr. Dale's one great theme; and there and then began the custom of singing in Carr's Lane on every Sunday morning an Easter hymn. The minister testified: "I want my people to get hold of the glorious fact that Christ is alive, and to rejoice over it; and Sunday, you know, is the day on which Christ left the grave."

ANONYMOUS

Eternity a Circle

The Christian Easter is not only historic fact but eternal reality which includes the facts of nature and history. A biologist, who is primarily a Christian and therefore is living creatively, said to me: "Eternity is a circle; a circle has no beginning and no ending; but a circle has a center, and the center is God." This spiritually geometrical figure is what is meant by the Easter Eternal. Like a circle, it is unbeginning and unending in the sense that it roots in the nature and purpose of God. Like a circle, also, it has its center in God, and is the only formula of God that is adequate for human beings to grasp and be grasped by—God in Christ.

FREDERICK F. SHANNON

Something Beyond

Someone tells of the great medieval altars built with panels, on both sides of which were paintings of Biblical scenes. One altar represents on the outside a very depressing portrayal of the Crucifixion. Against this dark background the heavy cross bears the lifeless body of the Christ. But on one side stands a figure with an outstretched arm indicating that there is something beyond, something not now seen. As a response to this urge, the panels are flung open and there is a flood of light and color and, in the center, is the radiant figure of the Risen and Triumphant Christ.

On Good Friday there is darkness covering the face of the land; hopes are blasted; dreams are shattered; it all seems like a lost cause. But on Good Friday we realize that there is something beyond, something not then seen by mortal man. It is the Easter morn, the empty tomb, the Risen Christ who abides with us always.

C. WESLEY ISRAEL

The Final Word

A journalist tells of listening to a Russian lecturer in Moscow who attacked the Christian faith for ninety minutes and proved to his own satisfaction that faith in God was a dying survival of capitalism. When he had finished he invited discussion. A timid young man—a typical village priest—stepped forward and asked permission to speak. "Not more than five minutes," the speaker reminded him. "I shall not be so long," replied the priest. He addressed the audience: "Brothers and sisters, Christ is risen!" As one man the audience replied, "He is risen indeed!"—the familiar response of Russian believers. "I have finished," said the priest, "I have nothing more to say."

ROLAND E. TURNBULL

Unless Easter Is True

Unless Easter is true, then Christ died in vain, his authority is shattered, and the church has been founded on a farce. Then his agony and work are sheer mockery, then the universe is a hollow echoing hell of demons; then men are motivated by something beyond their created environment that cynically mocks their hopes. If Easter be not true, then life is a farce and those who dared in his name are fools.

But Easter is true! It is truer than we are, for it is the last and ultimate fact about life and the world. Easter is God! The struggle is worth while! And though the world judge us fools, we glory in our foolishness, because to every believing person it is the wisdom and the power of God. We know in faith that Christ is the truth about life, that God is in the midst of life. In him the world coheres. He is promise and he is hope. In him is the centrifugal power which moves the whole creation toward himself.

E. G. HOMRIGHAUSEN

Hallelujahs Above the Wreckage

A friend of mine was in France during the Second World War and on Easter Day he attended a service in a little evangelical church. They came to church, those people of France, to find comfort; and they found it. At this service they were mostly old men, women, and children. The young and middle-aged men were dead or in some unknown prison camp. The bodies of those who were there were thin from hunger. Their eyes were ringed with darkness. They were ill-clad. Their land was in bondage. Yet they sang! They sang with fervor, "Christ the Lord is risen today, hallelujah!" My friend said: "As they sang there came into that group a strange, strong power, the power of the risen Christ, and I felt with them that no matter how dark the present might be or the future might become, there was still the strength of the risen Christ, that victory which overcomes the world."

JOHN E. SKOGLUND

The Easter Gospel

To live so that death is only an incident in the progress of an ever enlarging life! That is the possibility which is held out in the Easter Gospel, for that Gospel tells us of the risen Lord who is ready to live in us, so that our own living may have a beauty of its own. Yes, from self-distrust, from the world's disintegration and defeat, from the fear of death and from the dread of life, there is a way out and a way ahead.

WALTER RUSSELL BOWIE

Death a Sunrise

The earliest Gospel record of the resurrection story says of Mary and her two companions: "They went to the tomb when the sun had risen." We commonly associate

death with darkness and tombs with shadows and gloom.
We speak of old age as the twilight of life. Even our
hymns use the symbolism of night in treating of death:

> "Abide with me, fast falls the eventide,
>   The darkness deepens, Lord, with me abide."

Or again:

> "Though like a wanderer, the sun gone down,
>   Darkness be over me, my rest a stone."

Easter is a festival of dawn; yet, despite all the hosan-
nas of this joyous morning, we still talk and sing of death
as a sunset rather than a daybreak. Can we so take the
message of Easter to heart that we shall feel like Clement
of Alexandria when he said, "Christ hath turned our sunset into sunrise"?

RALPH W. SOCKMAN

The Significance of Easter

Easter marks the dawn of a new day. There is a vast
difference between another day and a new day. Another
day is a repetition, a mechanical affair. To count time by
saying, "Well, here is another day," is like turning a
crank and out come the days—one day, another day, another, and another; and on through threescore years and
ten. Something happened on Easter morn that changed
humanity's attitude toward time. Henceforward, every-

one who believes in Christ approaches time with an entirely new spirit and attitude. And the new experiences that were made possible by that Easter event are waiting for all, young and old, who will claim them.

BRUCE S. WRIGHT

Tomorrow Is Secure

Caught up by the Easter hallelujah, we see a new morning dawn. Tomorrow is secure, and today can be filled with the adventure of Christian living.

ROBERT MERRILL BARTLETT

The Easter Window

The Resurrection was the window through which the first disciples looked back upon their experience in companionship with Jesus. They had been confused and baffled by Jesus' teaching, his manner of life, and finally by his crucifixion. Their confusion arose on the one hand from their devoted attachment to him and the expectancy which he aroused in them, and on the other hand, from his strange behavior which seemed to belie their hopes. His death left them in utter despair. They returned to their homes and their nets. But his reappearance opened their eyes. They now saw all that occurred in a new light. Everything fell into a pattern. God had actually *sent* Jesus, they said, and all that had happened was revelatory. The teaching of Jesus was now seen as the law of God's kingdom. His love was seen as the unique manifestation of the love of God. His death on the cross was seen as the unveiling of God's own vicarious and redemptive suffering in and for man's sin. And the resurrection itself was seen as God's pledge that the meanings which they saw in these events were true.

Thus it is no exaggeration to say that Christianity became a living faith because of the Resurrection. I am not concerned to know the precise nature of this resurrection fact—whether the physical body of Jesus was resuscitated or whether he appeared in some other form. There are divergencies in the account. On the whole, I stand with Paul who denied the resuscitation concept and based his argument upon the concept of a "spiritual" body. Paul's statement is earlier than our earliest Gospel. But the manner of the Resurrection is not important. The fact of the Resurrection is supremely important, and the fact cannot be denied.

CHARLES CLAYTON MORRISON

An Act of Faith

The belief in the resurrection of Jesus is an act of faith; yes, it is, a faith in the justice, the reasonableness, the goodness, the squareness of the moral universe.

GEORGE CRAIG STEWART

Christianity's Symbols

The true symbol of Christianity is the empty cross, and indeed the empty tomb. No two-dimensional view known to man is adequate to send men hopefully to die or even to suffer unto death for righteousness and truth. Yet, with the perspective which Jesus gives us through the Cross one may and should look forward to death as a fitting climax to the Christian life on earth.

RAYMOND W. ALBRIGHT

Easter's Touch of Glory

Life can be, and is for many people, a mere existence. It becomes a matter of endless routine; we rise, eat, go to market, wash the dishes, sleep, and occasionally play; and then we do them all over again. Living can be a very dull, humdrum, and enervating experience. Someone has recorded that there are three great experiences in this world. The first is birth; the second, death; and the third, an inner experience somewhere between birth and death when one comes to a realization of the meaning of life. It is a time when there is a discovery of why you are here, where you are going, and what is the purpose of your life. Unless you have this truly spiritual experience you do not really live; you merely exist.

Easter is necessary to give a touch of glory to life. With this faith we are brought into new realms of beauty; we are given an understanding of the divine possibilities within the human breast. Easter, with its deeper meanings, saves us from deadening monotony. We see that "life is more than meat and the body more than raiment"; we behold anew that we are sons and daughters of the living God.

C. WESLEY ISRAEL

The Joy of Easter

On each new Easter there are gay colors and spring flowers and brave songs and fresh hope in men's hearts because early in the morning on the first Easter Day, when hope had been despaired of, the Conqueror over death came striding down the garden at sunrise. Death could not hold him. Death, thou shalt die! That is the Christian gospel. You may doubt the truth of all this, but please do not say that it doesn't matter one way or the other whether or not Jesus Christ rose from the tomb. It matters supremely. If Christ be not risen the faith of millions is vain and the victorious mission to which our belief commits us seems too big a proposition for unaided and unredeemed humanity.

But to many simple people, of whom I am one, the one great proof that Jesus Christ is alive comes out of the necessities of their own souls. We believe because we need and we believe because we know. We are delivered from discussion by yielding to devotion. It is like this:

"Then into his hand went mine,
And into my heart came he,
And I walk in a light divine
The path that I feared to see."

H. R. L. SHEPPARD

Easter a Turning Point in History

This is our eternal message: our Christ lives, conqueror of death. Here is the foundation of our hope and faith. From this point in time when God lived among men and conquered for them, all history is understood and judged. We do not look forward to some future revelation from God for victory, as do the Jews. Nor, as Christians, is our central point of hope based upon some future eschatological expectation. Christ, the Cross, and the Resurrection are the basis of our hope. Easter signifies death's defeat. Our redemption has been won, once and for all!

GORDON A. STOLTZ

Two Views—Take Your Choice

Easter is a symbol. It sets one interpretation of life over against another. Here is one interpretation—from a famous philosopher, Jean Paul Richter: "There is no God. I have traversed the worlds, I have risen to the suns, I have passed athwart the great waste places of the sky.

There is no God. I have descended to the place where the very shadow cast by being dies out and ends. I have gazed into the gulf beyond and cried, 'Father, where art thou?' But no answer came, save the sound of the storm which rages uncontrolled. We are orphans, you and I. Every soul in this vast corpse-trench of the universe is utterly alone."

And here is another interpretation, from the faith side. It is a paragraph from a letter in which one of the bravest souls in the world, Scott the explorer, wrote from his tent in the Antarctic concerning his companion, Dr. Edward Wilson: "If this letter reaches you, Bill and I will have gone out together. We are very near it now, and I should like you to know how splendid he was at the end—everlastingly cheerful and ready to sacrifice for others. Never a word of blame to me for leading him into this mess. His eyes have a comfortable blue look of hope, and his mind is peaceful in regarding himself as part of the great scheme of the Almighty."

Think of that brave spirit, having fought and lost on the wastes of the Antarctic, dying with his companions, his eyes with a "comfortable blue look of hope," and his mind at peace in regarding himself as part of the great scheme of the Almighty. To pass from Jean Paul Richter to Dr. Edward Wilson is to pass from death unto life; and to be dying in a tent in the Antarctic with that "comfortable blue look of hope" and a mind at peace is to be living under the spell of immortality.

ERNEST MARSHALL HOWSE

If a Man Die—

Easter answers the ever persistent question, "If a man die, shall he live again?" The glory of Easter is the risen Christ: "Because I live, ye too shall live." No philosophical treatise here, but a Risen Lord. And he goes before us—"Lo, I am with you alway, even unto the end of the world."

C. WESLEY ISRAEL

The Wonderful Window

There is an enchanting story called "The Wonderful Window." It is the tale of a London clerk, working in drab and depressing surroundings, who bought a mysterious oriental window and installed it high in his office workroom. Looking through this window, the hard-driven clerk saw not the familiar scenes of slums, sunless streets, dingy marts, and surly men, which had all but overwhelmed his soul. He saw rather a fairy city with beautiful castles and towers, green parks, wide streets, lovely homes, and happy people. On the highest tower there was a large white banner with a sturdy knight protecting the fair city from a fierce dragon of degeneracy and wrong. This wonderful window put a halo of glory on the everyday task for the young man of London town. Somehow he felt, as he added his long column of figures and painfully tried to make accounts balance, that he was working for that knight on the banner. Into his soul there came a sense of glamour and beauty. His part was to help the knight keep the city happy and beautiful and prosperous and strong.

The story of Easter, with its bright message of resurrection, is God's wonderful window of divine surprise.

CARL KNUDSEN

More Than an Event

The Resurrection was more than an event; it was the beginning of something new—a new message of hope and love to the world, a new courage and dynamic for the proclamation of that message and for the embodiment in constructive programs for the weal of human society, and a new way of life for the individuals who commit themselves to the leadership of that Master and to the comradeship of those who form the company of his followers.

CHARLES CLAYTON MORRISON

"When Life Tumbles In"

Of course there is grief. We would be less than human if hearts did not seem to break when life tumbles in. Let us accept the darkness for the moment, but keep our eyes keen to catch the first signs of dawn. We have a heartening example in a great Scottish preacher, Dr. Arthur Gossip of Aberdeen. His wife, who had long shared the responsibilities of a great city parish with him, died suddenly. There was no warning, no time to prepare for the change, no time to think through all the readjustments which would have to be made. Suddenly she slipped away, leaving behind her an almost intolerable loneliness. That was Tuesday. On Sunday, Dr. Gossip did not seek to be excused from his pulpit. He took his post as usual and preached one of the most searching and helpful sermons his people had ever heard. He took for his subject, "When Life Tumbles In, What Then?" Hundreds of men and women were given new courage by what he did and said that day.

A crushed life is a poor tribute to love. Easter says to us: There is a new day ahead. There is twilight, to be sure, but it is the twilight of the dawn. Courage! Take up the duty that lies nearest you! Believe that death is just an incident in the onward march of life!

M. H. LICHLITER

Comfort from the Resurrection

If there exists a single historical verity; if it is certain that Caesar crossed the Rubicon, and that Bonaparte died at St. Helena, it is certain that the message "Christ is risen" has been proclaimed by Christendom from the day when Peter the boatman harangued the crowds in Jerusalem to our own times, when this message is sent back by all the echoes of the globe. That is a fact. Men may seek to explain it in various ways; but who can contradict it? And who can deny that the message of the Resurrection has consoled many hearts, and raised heavenward many eyes sadly cast downward?

A. NAVILLE

The Best of All Human Dreams

Easter is consecrated to the dazzling triumph of Jesus over death. Everywhere, on Easter Day, altars are drifted with lilies, and choirs sing alleluias. But for many the idea of immortality swims in the ether of imagination, like Aladdin's palace, without rational support. And despite a cultural realism which catalogues such a belief with fairy tales, they wish it might be true and think it ought to be true. The unspoken litany of Easter is, "Lord, I believe, help thou mine unbelief."

But think of the Easter theme from Jesus' point of view. He said "that they might have life, and that more abundantly." He believed that immortality is a normal outgrowth of life—life with ever expanding and enriching meanings—and that every man should be able to say, "I am the resurrection," before he looks the physical experience of death in the face. That is what Jesus means by "life more abundant." And that is why he gave incentive to this the best of all human dreams.

SAMUEL HARKNESS

The Radiant Portal

Dim gray dawn lay on Gethsemane that first Easter morning. Then suddenly a light shone through the grayness! Not the sun breaking over the horizon. Not the lantern of the guards around a tomb. It came from the door of the sepulcher itself, shining with a dazzling glory. And when Christ stepped out through that open doorway from death into life, he showed us the way of the radiant portal into life everlasting.

ESTHER BALDWIN YORK

Difficult Not to Believe

Modern people try not to believe. They try to set aside the conviction that for ages has been an irrepressible affirmation of the human spirit, expressed by the simplest of God's children in the most unlettered tribes, and by the mightiest intellects that have ever grappled with the issues of life and death, from Plato to St. Paul, from Kant to Lord Kelvin and Eddington and Compton. They construct laborious arguments against it, they elaborate skepticisms to disprove it. They attempt vainly to convince their own minds that Isaiah and Beethoven, Wycliffe and Wesley, and that dear soul whom you have loved and lost a while, are no more than a dollar's worth of chemicals, which happened for a transient day to be arranged in a particular pattern that produced an illusion—a pattern of no more significance than the next that will produce a clod of earth or a skylark, a snow-flake or a desert weed. Small wonder that at times they cannot help doubting their unbelief, that they cannot help wondering whether the perishable values of the dust can comprise all the imperishable values of the spirit.

On Easter Day the strongest doubts within us are the doubts of our unbelief. The light of Easter dawn far out-shines the poet's pale "sunset touch"; and more miracu-lously than the rays which leap the solar spaces, its un-fading afterglow spans the centuries with a splendor which brightens our souls as we repeat the ancient affir-mation of St. Paul: "This mortal nature must put on im-mortality." In that faith on Easter Day we dignify our lives, we ground our character, we assert our hope in-vincible. It is beyond our reason to speak but it is not beyond our feelings to sing: "Hallelujah! The Lord God Omnipotent reigneth!"

ERNEST MARSHALL HOWSE

"He Is Risen!"

"He is not here, for Christ has risen and goeth before you into Galilee." He is not here, but is risen and goeth before you into your homes and factories, into your shops and places of business, into your labor and pleas-ure, into your family and friendships. Gone before you into all the rich variety of human activity that you may

be redeemed from frustration, despair, and leanness of
soul. Turn toward the dawn and see the radiant light of
life eternal streaming across the darkened world. It is
the risen Christ revealing the glory of the Life Everlasting.

HAROLD E. MARTIN

"There Is More Day to Dawn"

Oliver Cromwell on his deathbed, hearing the weeping
of his friends, roused himself and cried, "Is there no one
here who will praise God?" Confusion and difficulty
surge about us; is there no one who will praise God and
stir the soul of humanity with hope? "Only the day
dawns to which we awake. There is more day to dawn.
The sun is but a morning star."

This morning of the soul offers to us its victorious
truth about the unknown tomorrow and about the perplexing today. Whatever our cross, we can be caught up
up to new levels, like the bell ringer in Korolenko's Russian story. On Easter the old man went into the steeple
of the church where he had proudly rung the bells for
many years. He could scarcely mount the stairs because
of age and illness. He prayed that God might permit him
to ring out the resurrection song over the earth once
more. From the belfry he looked down upon the graveyard and the sleeping village. Murmuring "All glory be
to God," he took hold of the ropes and began to ring

out the song, "Christ is risen." His weariness and weakness left him, and he was transported by the magic of its melody. His old heart forgot about life, full of cares and wrongs. He forgot that life had become for him a thing shut up in a melancholy tower; he forgot that he was alone in the world—like an old stump, weatherbeaten and broken.

The music blended into one great chorus, and sang to him of joyousness, which he had not before tasted. And the old man continued to tug at the ropes, while tears ran down his face, and his heart trembled with happiness. And the people cried: "Never before have we heard the message of Easter played with such beauty"— as the old bell ringer took his hands from the ropes and fell exhausted on the bench, while his last tears trickled down his pale face.

And we, caught up by the Easter hallelujah, see a new morning dawn. Tomorrow is secure, and today can be filled with the adventure of Christian living. The Eternal Christ stands before us, within the halo of adoring centuries, and salutes us with the joy-word of the ages, "Hail!" "Be of good cheer! I have overcome the world!"

ROBERT MERRILL BARTLETT

If No Resurrection?

If Christ be not risen, perhaps agnosticism is best. Without the Resurrection man's future is shrouded in fog. Of

course, throughout the history of the race you find this
hope of immortality. Men everywhere have been able to
say with Victor Hugo, "I feel immortality within myself." But what if that is a delusion? Muriel Lester tells
us that her brother so strongly desired to believe in a
future life that he couldn't. "My wishes," he said, "make
me distrust my judgment."

But if, indeed, Christ is risen, this life which we have
begun with him is eternal. We are to be with him, and to
be like him. This is his promise, and to it his resurrection
gives the great Amen!

W. TALIAFERRO THOMPSON

Eternity in Time

Easter, when it is understood at its highest, turns our
minds from what may or may not be beyond the grave
to a quality of life which can never be buried at all. That
is what the Resurrection really means, that there was in
Jesus Christ a quality of life which was deathless. What
became of his body does not matter. As Dean Inge has
said with great common sense, "It is impossible to prove
that a tomb was empty nineteen centuries ago, and even
if it could be proved, we should be unable to show that
all alternative suggestions were impossible." We come
back to the essential truth, that eternity is something we
may experience now and here, and any rational vista of
eternity should comprehend those present spiritual

values in our lives which cannot possibly die. "Ye are come . . . to the spirits of just men made perfect." There is a communion of saints, there is a vital fellowship of spirits which absolutely transcends the incident of death. There is such a thing as eternity in time.

M. H. Lichliter

The Grave Is Incidental

The outward accompaniments of the Resurrection are secondary, but, because of man's incurable materialism, are most dwelt upon. Possibly an angel or an earthquake moved the stone—it doesn't matter much; it was moved not to let Jesus out but to let the disciples in. The grave could not hold him. In fact, according to Scripture, our Lord did not stay in the grave but went preaching to the souls in prison; and when the time came for him to resume his body he went through the sealed entrance of the tomb as easily as he went through the closed doors where the disciples and apostles were assembled on that first night. The grave is a coarse thing; it cannot hold a spiritual being. As Pilate is reputed to have said: "I cannot kill him, empires cannot kill him, he is alive!" Socrates answered when asked, "What shall we do with you when you are dead?"—"Anything you like, if you can catch me." So it was not so much a miraculous thing as a natural and inevitable thing.

G. Ashton Oldham

"Explaining" the Resurrection

Can you explain a genius like Einstein, or Milton, or Jesus? You cannot see how, beyond the grave, the spirit, soul, personality recognizes, comprehends, communicates, enjoys, or achieves. No, you cannot explain it. But can you explain how a voice goes over the ether waves and is heard around the world, instantaneously? Even after the technician has "explained" it all to us, the radio still astounds and mystifies us. There are mysteries of this universe too great for our finite minds to grasp. So, it is sheer folly to disbelieve in immortality because we cannot explain it.

C. WESLEY ISRAEL

The Real Test of Christ—He Lives!

Christ is not pre-eminently the Son of God because he was born of a virgin. He is not pre-eminently the Son of God because he rose from the dead. I believe he did, with all my soul, but if you ask me to explain it, I cannot. But of one thing I am sure: Christ lives! He lives forever. He could not die. He had such a grip upon the life of God that he knew men could not stop it, could not dam it up. He knew he was eternal, because to him God was life. "He is not the God of the dead, but of the living."

FREDERICK W. NORWOOD

The Cross—and Beyond

I cannot see how Christians can be satisfied with the crucifix as a symbol of our faith. How can we keep perpetually before our eyes the dying Christ, the Christ still bound to the cross, and at the same time sing the Easter hymns, hear the reading of the Easter story, read again our Lord's words, "Because I live, ye shall live also"? I would not for a moment do away with the cross as a Christian symbol. But I would shout from the housetops that it is an empty cross, a cross from which the Christ has gone; a cross which he has left behind forever.

ELMER S. FREEMAN

The Challenge of Easter

Let me put before you the real challenge of Easter. Do you think the Easter question for you is the question of your belief as to what lies beyond death? Do you think it has to do with ghosts and psychical research and that sort of thing? I tell you no. This business of rising from the dead is first of all a matter of being alive. If you are not rising from the dead now, you never will. Instead of speculating about the future life, we had better face the question whether we ourselves may not be already among the unburied dead.

That is where this Easter question becomes a personal

one and puts us all on the carpet. Not your theoretical beliefs about God and Christ. Not your conventional morals. But the quality of your inner being as evidenced in your response to life. Are we keeping our hearts open with love and sympathy? Are we keeping our minds fresh and eager? Are we making our lives an adventure in knowledge and freedom and loving service? Are we meeting our situations in such a way as to emerge continually into fuller understanding and fellowship and joy?

That is what rising from the dead means. To be like a tree that grows a new and larger ring every year. To be like a Sequoia Sempervirens: you can cut it down but you can't kill it; from its roots there springs a circle of young trees around the old stump.

The sign of life is growth—no growth, no life. That is what Easter means.

WILLARD B. THORP

Shining Sentences

Those who hope for no other life are dead even in this.

J. W. VON GOETHE

After the sun is down, and the west faded, the heavens begin to fill with stars.

ROBERT LOUIS STEVENSON

The seed dies into a new life, and so does man.

GEORGE MacDONALD

Death? Translated into the heavenly tongue, that word means life!

HENRY WARD BEECHER

There is nothing innocent or good that dies and is forgotten: let us hold to that faith or none.

CHARLES DICKENS

Easter Means Triumph

The Easter life is a triumphant life, so radiant that it is worth going on with always. The eternal life into which Christian faith calls you is the present sharing of the goodness, truth, and beauty of God's creative life. It isn't a weird sort of existence—a floating about on a cloud, plucking a harp forever. You might get that impression from "The Green Pastures" or from the man on the street, but you will never get that conception from the New Testament or from St. John!

The Christian message of Easter dare not be misunderstood as an effort to prove existence after death, or as the assertion of empty immortality, or as the promise of future reward. The message of Easter expressed in the words of Jesus speaks directly to our mood. It says: When life is lived with God in Christ it cannot be defeated. If your life expresses the purposes and shares the spirit of God, it cannot conclude with death or disaster. Life in God triumphs over death because God's life knows not defeat nor death. You are now participating in this abundant or eternal life if your purposes and spirit are in Jesus Christ. "I am the life. . . . No one who is alive and believes in me will ever die." I ask you, as Jesus did: Do you believe that?

CHARLES W. KEGLEY

Resurrection Made Real

For those whose religion is a thing of codes, of gifts and rewards, whose thinking is concerned with material things, who are of the earth earthy, to speak of a resurrection is an irrelevance; for in their opinion there is nothing to survive. But those whose eyes are opened to behold things invisible and unseen, whose thoughts dwell on things above, seekers after truth, strivers after goodness, well may shout with Saint Paul his triumphant challenge to the powers of darkness: "O death, where is thy sting? O grave, where is thy victory?"

G. ASHTON OLDHAM

The Resurrection Assurance

No, heaven and hell are still mysteries, only hinted at in the religious experiences of life. But if our freedom, however limited, is real, and we are the kind of creatures made in the image of God the Bible says we are, then this much is certain: there is a heaven of living by God's will revealed in the life and death and resurrection of Jesus Christ, and there is a hell of rebellion against his will. And it is the Resurrection that is witness to the fact that those who surrender to this will are assured of a continuance of life with him in eternity, beyond history, in a kingdom not made with hands, high and lifted up.

J. CLAUDE EVANS

Ground of the Christian Hope

The foremost ground of the Christian hope is the resurrection of Christ. The rising again of their Master from the grave was the event that first begot in the disciples a lively hope of resurrection from the dead. He had overcome death; he could not be holden by it; he was living in the power of an endless life; and by his rising again he had abolished death and brought life and immortality to light. "But now," cries Paul, "is Christ risen from the dead, and become the first fruits of them that slept." And again, "God both raised the Lord and will raise up us through his power." That is the Christian faith. And what a faith it is!

ROBERT J. MCCRACKEN

HEAVEN—THE "OTHER ROOM"

Only a Step to a Greater World

HEAVEN—THE "OTHER ROOM"

"*A Bigger, Brighter Room*"

Shall I doubt my Father's mercy?
Shall I think of death as doom,
Or the stepping o'er the threshold
To a bigger, brighter room?

ROBERT FREEMAN

"*Safe at Home*"

The Christian is convinced that the true experiences of life are spiritual, a world within, unseen and unseeable. When we come to the great hour, we have faith that death will not sever the ties which bind our spirits to God and to the spiritual world within. An anxious person once asked Bishop Berggrav of Norway his view of death. The bishop replied with this story:

"One day a peasant took his little son with him on a visit to a village some distance away. Along the road they came to a swift stream which was spanned by a rickety old bridge. But it was daylight and the father and son made the crossing without mishap. It was dusk when the two started on their homeward journey. The boy remembered the stream and the old bridge, and became frightened. How would they be able to cross that turbulent stream in the dark? His father, noticing his anxiety, lifted him up and carried him in his arms. The lad's fear subsided immediately, and before the boy knew it he was fast asleep on his father's shoulder. As the sun of a new day streamed through the window of his bedroom, the boy awoke and discovered that he was safe at home."

Death is like that to the Christian. What we dread most, the river of death, we are able to cross unafraid, falling asleep in the arms of the Father. Soon we awake in the Father's house of many mansions, where there is no night and no fear.

CHARLES R. WOODSON

The House Not Made with Hands

In the midst of our most active duties, when life seems most full of joy and richest in satisfactions, it is always well to pause and reflect upon the life immortal. This we should do not to counteract our natural zest for this

life, but rather to increase it, and to let the light of the
Beyond flow in upon us here. To the Christian, the
thought of the House not made with hands, nor standing upon the foundations of human vicissitude, is a
thought that inspires joy and hope and fills the heart
with song.

HERBERT L. WILLETT

Not the Rest of Idleness

Said Marshal Foch to the priest who stood by his side
when he was dying: "I have had my span of life. All
I want now is heaven." How right that is! The pathos
and simplicity of a little child is in it, and yet the gal-
lantry of a warrior, too. We may recognize that the
span of this life is done. But if life has meant anything
great and purposeful, we are reaching out to a heaven
which lies beyond. Granted that this word has been cari-
catured so that many almost affect to despise it. Granted
that religious symbolism has been turned into a mawkish
sentimentality, so that people have talked of heaven as
though it meant nothing except white robes and palms
and harps and a kind of saccharine happiness in general.
Yet the heaven toward which the reality of our souls
reaches out is not like that. It is rest, but not the rest of
idleness. Rather is it the movement of increasing life
which has found its center and its rest in God.

WALTER RUSSELL BOWIE

Home!

Think of stepping on shore, and finding it Heaven!
Of taking hold of a hand, and finding it God's hand,
Of breathing new air, and finding it celestial air,
Of feeling invigorated, and finding it immortality,
Of passing from storm and tempest to an unbroken
   calm,
Of waking up, and finding it Home!

ANONYMOUS

The Meaning of Heaven

There is a realm in life where there is neither coming
nor going. There is a realm in life where the constant
and never ceasing flowing of things comes to an end
and all is gathered up in a moment of being. It is something that is there, something that *is*. Children always
ask the question, Where does the wind go? Where *does*
it go? Well, the answer is that it does not go anywhere.
It *is*. It whips up and it dies down, but the wind is.
Where does a good man go when he dies? He does not
go, he is! What is once done is done and nothing can
gainsay it. A relationship once lived is lived. It is the time
when time stands still. We get flashes of it, every now
and then, in great music when we are not conscious of
development or movement, but simply an intimation that
there is something, a presence, with which a calendar
has nothing to do.

I admit that that is poor language. I do not know how else to say it. It is what the Bible means by heaven. It is what the first Christians were trying to say in their rather clumsy way—to us modern astronomers—when they said that a cloud received him out of their sight as he ascended into heaven. They meant that he had not really gone away anywhere, that he simply is—and we can be with him everlastingly, always everywhere; that he belongs to that realm of eternal abiding reality in which time moves, but against which time can make no final destructive movement.

THEODORE P. FERRIS

Heaven Is Growth in Love

"If ye are risen with Christ seek those things that are above." Why fritter away our existence in aimless and valueless pursuits if we can feed the deep springs of eternal life and live on the heights? Rufus Jones goes so far as to say that "hell consists only in being eternally what you are." Are we satisfied with what we are? Then we are preparing for an uncomfortable and distressing existence in the future. But heaven is growth in the love for truth, in the capacity for higher fellowship, in love for God and service to man. Why not, then, break away from our aboriginal bondage to the physical, to the selfish, to the narrow satisfactions and begin to live the life of quality and spiritual enhancement?

CARL KNUDSEN

Not an Endless Church Service

In a letter to a London paper, George Bernard Shaw said it would be a dreadful calamity indeed to have this thing called Shaw go on forever, pouring out thousands of plays and millions of articles. He felt that a time would come when he would want to go on his knees before God and ask if there was not some way of bringing this insufferable process to an end. But he said he could not conceive of personal immortality at all, unless in terms of going on just as now.

Jesus, however, offers a heaven which shall be the prolonging of the work begun here on a higher plane. The old idea of heaven as a kind of endless church service has lost its appeal in this modern age. The hymn which described heaven as a place "where congregations ne'er break up and sabbaths have no end" is not sung much in these days. As Ian Maclaren says, "Heaven is not a Trappist monastery; neither is it retirement on a pension. No, it is a land of continual progress." There is one translation of Jesus' familiar promise to the disciples which is very attractive. Instead of making him say "In my Father's house are many mansions," this newer translation has him say "In my Father's house are many *stations*." The word "stations" implies progress. If this reading is correct, what an endless opportunity for adventurous and abundant living! What an encouragement to all the lives which never "arrived" on earth, to all who were cut off before the song was sung and the picture painted and the vision realized!

Cheer up, beloved! Somewhere the ragged edges of our earthy work will be taken up and woven into a better pattern.

HERBERT BOOTH SMITH

Jasper Walls and a Great White Throne?

All the greatest souls of the race have believed and said: "I shall not die." But Jesus, who was perfectly sure of the Beyond, avoided all description. While certain of the "many mansions," he used none of the architectural imagery of the Book of Revelation or of "Pilgrim's Progress." Jasper walls and a great white throne and crowns and harps had no meaning for the Nazarene and can have none for us. "Where I am there shall my servant be" is enough to know. All talk of golden streets simply cheapens our faith in the future. Nothing do we need but eternal companionship and co-operation with God in the divine adventure of creation.

W. H. P. FAUNCE

Not Gold Streets

Heaven as a place of gold streets, pearly gates, and harp playing has very little appeal to most men if they are honest. Dante tried to picture such a place, but, great poet that he was, he is much more interesting when he talks about Purgatory than he is when talking about the perfect finality of Paradise; for those who are in his Purgatory still look forward to growth. Unless all of our deepest experience of religion is misleading, heaven will be a place where those impulses and longings dimly felt but never realized shall be made possible of fulfillment

GERALD KENNEDY

They Are Ever with Us

If we were to permit ourselves to regard death narrowly, as a solitary and appalling fact, we should feel hopelessly separated from those whom we love who have taken the hand of death and left us alone. But viewed in the broader sense, this experience is an onward step in the ceaseless progress of the soul toward completion. Our beloved are not far from us, and are busy at some of the worthful tasks of our Father's universe. In that wider companionship they are ever with us.

HERBERT L. WILLETT

The Secret of Her Courage

I believe we shall know our loved ones better in the spirit realm than here. A widow who had come so bravely through the loss of her beloved husband was asked the secret of her sublime courage. Listen to her answer:

"Here is one thing that has been a great joy to me. I know him better than I ever knew him before. It is not just that the daily preoccupations and absorptions and all the little rough edges that everybody has keep us from fully knowing each other while we are alive, here, together. It is partly that, but also something else. It is that you are too close to the picture, you don't see the whole—the details occupy you too much. And the canvas isn't complete, anyway. Death completes it. You step back from the picture then, you see it as a whole, and you find beauties in it that escaped you when you were so near it, when it was in the making."

RALPH W. SOCKMAN

What Heaven Will Mean

It is an end of pain, or travail and sorrow, of doubt and hesitation and fear. It is peace and rest and calm—and reunion with those we have lost a while. We shall know each other there far better than we ever knew each other here. Spirit with spirit will meet, and we shall be closer than breathing, nearer than hands and feet.

BURRIS JENKINS

New Tasks in Heaven

It is impossible that we should think of our beloved dead as unconscious or unemployed. In the measure of the strength and skill for holy tasks which they gather in this life we may be confident that they are at work in some portion of the house not made with hands. To think otherwise would be to attribute a certain wastefulness to that divine administration of the universe whose highest law is service.

HERBERT L. WILLETT

The Instinct for Immortality

When William Blake, the poet, lay dying, he said he was going to that country he had wished to see all his life; and it is related that just before his death he burst into singing of the things he saw. Somehow, we all have the traveler's instinct and are never satisfied until we have visited the capitol of the soul-country which we familiarly call "heaven." As Paul said, "We must see Rome." When Charles Kingsley came to the last station on this side of the ferry—on his sickbed where he lay on the boundary between the two worlds—he cried out: "God forgive me, but I look forward to it with an intense and reverent curiosity."

Now, it may be remarked that the hope of a future life is an unprovable hypothesis, the fond dream of a disordered imagination; to which we reply that an instinct is part of our spiritual capital which antedates proof; and the two chief instincts of humanity are God and immortality. Surely we cannot drown an instinct as though its voice had no right to be heard; for instinct in its place is just as divinely planted as conscience. And God has not given us our instincts to deceive us or to lead us astray. The instinct of hunger or thirst; of fear, of love, of modesty; all these, when we follow them, bring us out on the right road. Why should we suppose that the instinct of futurity is a blind path which abruptly ends in the boundless forest at a signboard marked "Lost"? Nay, as Professor Fiske says, from the view of a trained thinker, this outreaching after the unseen is not mere idealism; for if it is, it is something utterly without precedent in the process of evolution. It must be the beckoning of a distinct land somewhere beyond the forest darkness. There must be a turn in the road somewhere; somewhere "the wicked cease from troubling and the weary are at rest."

HERBERT BOOTH SMITH

WE BELIEVE IN IMMORTALITY

A Chorus of Testimony

WE BELIEVE IN IMMORTALITY

"Is It a Dream? Nay . . ."

Is it a dream?
Nay, but the lack of it the dream,
And failing it life's lore and wealth a dream,
And all the world a dream.

WALT WHITMAN

"Yet Will I Trust Him"

I believe that man is made in the spiritual likeness of the
Eternal, and that life means an ever closer approximation
to the imperishable elements of life. I do not believe that
man is set upon the earth to rise to the sublimities of love
and truth and goodness by the hard, steep pathway of
their sacrificial quest—only to be doomed to extinction.

"Though he slay me, yet would I trust in him"; though
he seem not to answer my prayer, still let my Godward
soul reach up to the manward God. Summoned to be a
sharer in life's divine tasks and burdens, I believe that my
soul is to go on forever in the divine comradeship.

STEPHEN S. WISE

The Only Proof Needed

I believe in immortality because Jesus taught it and believed it. This is all the proof I need. This is the basis
of my knowledge and the beginning and end of all argument.

CHARLES M. SHELDON

More Important Than War!

During the First World War, Henri Bergson, the noted
French philosopher, and Lord Balfour came to America
to enlist the aid of America in the cause of the Allies.
After a meeting in New York, they retired to the home
of Joseph H. Choate where they engaged in a long discussion. Asked later the subject of their conversation, Mr.
Choate replied, "Immortality."

A. GORDON NASBY

Twilight—Dawn!

Winter is on my head, but eternal spring is in my heart. The nearer I approach the end, the plainer I hear around me the immortal symphonies of the world to come. I will not say when the last moment comes that I have finished my life. For half a century I have been writing my thoughts in prose and verse; but I feel that I have not said one-thousandth part of what is in me. When I have gone down to the grave I shall have ended one day's work; but another day will begin the next morning. Life closes in the twilight but opens with the dawn.

VICTOR HUGO

All Hope Rests in God

For myself, I ground all hope in God. Whether, therefore, we wake or sleep we are the Lord's. He gave us being, and if it shall so please him he will continue us in being the endless partakers of his life and joy. As old Marcus Aurelius said, "It is good to die if there is God, and sad to live if there is not." The whole question rests with our Maker, who is our Heavenly Father and whose character has been expressed with sovereign beauty and power by the Lord Jesus Christ.

GEORGE A. GORDON

One World at a Time

God is making the world, and the show is so grand and beautiful and exciting, I have never been able to study any other. Nor do I fret about this ignorance of future life, being willing to take one world at a time, since the Lord of this is also Lord of every other. And surely none who has enjoyed God's glory and goodness on earth need look forward to any other without boundless trust and a thankful heart.

JOHN MUIR

What the Great Ones Say

Bergson, the French philosopher, though not a Christian, declared: "I firmly believe that we maintain our individuality after death." Evan Tyndall, scientist and rationalist, said that "only in dull, depressing moments does this faith lose its hold on the heart." . . . Is it necessary to cite the German poet Goethe, or the German philosopher Immanuel Kant, or the English poets of the Victorian era, Tennyson and Browning, or the greatest men of science of recent years, Sir Oliver Lodge, Sir Arthur Keith, Michael Pupin, Robert A. Millikan? Oh, the thinkers are legion who bear me company in a reasoned and reasonable faith that death is but an incident, only life's most beautiful adventure.

BURRIS JENKINS

The Mystery of Death

All the best and most beautiful flowers of character and thought seem to me to spring up in the track of suffering, and what is the most sorrowful of all mysteries, the mystery of death, the ceasing to be, the relinquishing of our hopes and dreams, the breaking of our dearest ties, becomes more solemn and awe-inspiring the nearer we advance to it.

A. C. BENSON

We Believe!

We believe that out of every grave there blooms an Easter lily, and in every tomb there sits an angel. We believe in a risen Lord. Turn not your faces to the past that you may worship only at his grave, but above and within that you may worship the Christ who lives. And because he lives, we shall live also.

LYMAN ABBOTT

Because We Believe It

We do not believe in immortality because we have proved it, but we forever try to prove it because we believe it.

JAMES MARTINEAU

What About Science?

Arthur H. Compton, renowned in the field of the physical sciences, testifies: "Science can neither prove nor disprove. But she is coming to show many considerations favorable to a belief in the future life."

Three Cheers!

Methinks we have hugely mistaken this matter of life and death. Methinks that what they call my shadow here on earth is my true substance. Methinks that in looking at things spiritual we are too much like oysters observing the sun through water, and thinking that thick water the thinnest of air. Methinks my body is but the lees of my being. In fact, take my body who will; take it, I say, it is not me. And therefore three cheers!

HERMAN MELVILLE

Beyond the Hills of Time

On his ninetieth birthday, Sir William Mullock, late Chief Justice of Canada and oldest judge in the British Empire, said: "I am still at work, and with my face to the future. The shadows of evening lengthen, but the morning is in my heart. The testimony I bear is this: the best of life is further on, hidden from our eyes beyond the hills of time."

The Immortal Hope

For my own part I believe in the immortality of the soul, not in the sense that I accept the demonstrable truths of science, but in the supreme act of faith in the reasonableness of God's work. Such a crown of wonder seems to me no more than the fit climax to a creative work that has been ineffably beautiful and marvelous in all its myriad stages.

JOHN FISKE

Socrates' Testimony

The great Greek philosopher, Socrates, had not the advantage of the light which came through the revelation of Christ, but he drank the hemlock in full faith that he would still live. He is quoted as saying: "Beyond question the soul is immortal and imperishable and will long exist in another world."

A Scientific Basis

As Darwin and his confreres found evolution, so man finds immortality. The thought of immortality is as well founded as any other well-authenticated postulate of the human reason.

JOHN HAYNES HOLMES

Through Death to Life

They that love beyond the world cannot be separated by
it. Death cannot kill what never dies. Nor can spirits
ever be divided that love and live in the same divine
principle: the root and record of their friendship. If
absence be not death, neither is theirs. Death is but crossing the world, as friends do the seas; they live in one
another still. For they must needs be present, that love
and live in that which is omnipresent.

WILLIAM PENN

Not at All Incredible

That we should survive death is not to me incredible. The
thing that is incredible is life itself. Why should there be
any life at all? Why should this world of stars have ever
come into existence? Why should you be here, why
should I be here this afternoon? Why should we be here
in this sun-illumined universe? Why should there be
green earth under our feet? How did all this happen?
This wonder that we know, this is the incredible thing.
What power projected it all into existence? This chal-
lenges my faith, excites my astonishment, lifts me to the
ineffable.

EDWIN MARKHAM

Facing Death Without Hope

How gloomy would be the mansions of the dead to him
who did not know that he should never die; that what
now acts, shall continue its agency, and what now thinks,
shall think on forever!

SAMUEL JOHNSON

The Idea of Immortality

We are no more responsible for the idea of immortality
in the heart than for the eye of physical vision in the
head.

KARL REILAND

I Believe in Heaven

I believe in heaven; not a heaven of literal golden streets,
walls of jasper, and gates of pearl, although I dearly love
to dream over such beautiful imagery. I believe in the
heaven of peace of mind and conscience that comes as a
result of endeavoring to do the will of God as exhibited
in the life and teachings of Jesus. I believe in the heaven
of comradeships of the like-minded here, and by and by
of the spirits of just men made perfect. I believe in the
heaven of high resolutions, noble dedications, grand
pioneering ventures, as one follows the Prince of Peace

and climbs "the steep ascent of heaven, through peril, toil, and pain," he follows in the train of the Son of God. And, if I may quote from an old revival hymn, "I'm living in heaven now."

EDGAR DEWITT JONES

Immortality Is Inevitable

I believe in immortality because I believe in the God of Christ. That such a God would call men into existence, mock them with a few draughts of life, and then let them perish, is incredible to me. The doctrine of God as Father means nothing to me without the possibility of the immortality of the sons of God. Once accept the Christ idea of God, and immortality seems to me to follow as a matter of moral inevitability.

FRANCIS J. McCONNELL

From Eternity to Eternity

When a man is as old as I am, he is bound occasionally to think about death. In my case this thought leaves me in perfect peace, for I have a firm conviction that our spirit is a being indestructible by nature. It works from eternity to eternity; it is like a sun which only seems to set, but in truth never sets but shines on unceasingly .

J. W. VON GOETHE

An Ancient Sage's View

This life is only a prelude to eternity. For that which we call death is but a pause, in truth a progress into life.

SENECA

Philosophers on Immortality

Many philosophers have proclaimed their faith in life beyond death with no reference to the resurrection of Jesus. Plato certainly believed in the future life, and Socrates probably did. And on occasion a Christian scientist-philosopher-theologian could argue for immortality with no reference to religious presuppositions. Listen to Pascal:

"Atheists: What right have they to say that one cannot rise from the dead? Which is the more difficult, to be born or to rise again; that which has never been, be, or that which has been, be again? Is it more difficult to come into being than to return to being? Custom makes the one seem easy, the absence of custom makes the other seem impossible: a popular method of judging."

Christians have taken the next step and have insisted that because Jesus lives, we also shall live again.

J. CLAUDE EVANS

Deathless Faith

When Victor Hugo was past eighty years of age he gave expression to his religious faith in these sublime sentences: "I feel in myself the future life. I am like a forest which has been more than once cut down. The new shoots are livelier than ever. I am rising toward the sky. The sunshine is on my head. The earth gives me its generous sap, but heaven lights me with its unknown worlds. You say the soul is nothing but the resultant of the bodily powers. Why, then, is my soul more luminous when my bodily powers begin to fail? I breathe at this hour the fragrance of the lilacs, the violets, and the roses as at twenty years."

That Great Day

When I look upon the tombs of the great, every emotion of envy dies in me; when I read the epitaphs of the beautiful, every inordinate desire goes out; when I meet with the grief of parents upon a tombstone, my heart melts with compassion; when I see the tomb of the parents themselves, I consider the vanity of grieving for those whom we must quickly follow: when I see kings lying by those who deposed them, or holy men who divided the world with their disputes, I reflect with sorrow on the little competitions and factions of mankind. When I read the several dates of the tombs, of some that died yesterday and some six hundred years ago, I consider that

Great Day when we shall all of us be contemporaries, and make our appearance together.

JOSEPH ADDISON

A Statesman's Creed

Here is my creed. I believe in one God, Creator of the universe. That he governs it by his Providence. That he ought to be worshiped. That the most acceptable service we render him is doing good to his other children. That the soul of man is immortal, and will be treated with justice in another life respecting its conduct in this.

BENJAMIN FRANKLIN

A Benignant Purpose

The fundamental reason for my faith in immortality is that I must think of the whole cosmic process as having some such meaning as is possessed by human creativity. I have a passionate belief that there is a benignant purpose in the great ongoing process. I find this meaning most immediately expressed in human personality in its finer reaches and I dare to believe that the universe has personal quality. I cannot think of this supreme value being anywhere destroyed.

THEODORE G. SOARES

An Impossible Conjecture

The thought of being nothing after death is a burden
insupportable to a virtuous man; we naturally aim at happiness and cannot bear to have it confined to our present
being.

JOHN DRYDEN

I Cannot Prove, but I Believe

I believe in the survival of human personality because I
believe that the universe is sufficiently intelligent to preserve its highest values. Truth, beauty, love, and goodness—these are values that ought to be conserved. On
this point there is, I take it, no difference of opinion. But
how can they be conserved unless certain gallant and
gracious personalities are preserved? Where do these supreme values reside? Only in persons and in personal
relationships. . . . The only way the universe can preserve its supreme values is to preserve human personality.
Will it be so? I cannot prove, but I believe, that it will.

ERNEST FREMONT TITTLE

TESTIMONY OF THE POETS

Dreamers Are the Best Interpreters

TESTIMONY OF THE POETS

"'Tis We Musicians Know"

Sorrow is hard to bear, and doubt is slow to clear,
   Each sufferer says his say, his scheme of the weal and
      woe;
But God has a few of us whom he whispers in the ear;
   The rest may reason and welcome; 'tis we musicians
     know.

ROBERT BROWNING

From *Threnody*

   Wilt thou not ope thy heart to know
   What rainbows teach, and sunsets show?
   Verdict which accumulates
   From lengthening scroll of human fates,
   Voice of earth to earth returned,

Prayers of saints that inly burned—
Saying, *What is excellent*
As God lives, is permanent;
Hearts are dust, hearts' loves remain;
Hearts' love will meet thee again.

RALPH WALDO EMERSON

Joy, Shipmate, Joy!

Joy, shipmate, joy!
(Pleased to my soul at death I cry),
Our life is closed, our life begins,
The long, long anchorage we leave,
The ship is clear at last, she leaps!
She swiftly courses from the shore,
Joy, shipmate, joy!

WALT WHITMAN

Epilogue

At the midnight in the silence of the sleep-time,
    When you set your fancies free,
Will they pass to where—by death, fools think, impris-
    oned—
Low he lies who once so loved you, whom you loved so,
            —Pity me?

Oh to love so, be so loved, yet so mistaken!
   What had I on earth to do
With the slothful, with the mawkish, the unmanly?
Like the aimless, helpless, hopeless did I drivel
               —Being—who?

One who never turned his back but marched breast
    forward,
   Never doubted clouds would break,
Never dreamed, though right were worsted, wrong
    would triumph,
Held we fall to rise, are baffled to fight better,
             Sleep to wake.

No, at noonday in the bustle of man's worktime
   Greet the unseen with a cheer!
Bid him forward, breast and back as either should be,
"Strive and thrive!" cry, "Speed—fight on, fare ever
          There as here!"

                           ROBERT BROWNING

Is This the End?

Is this the end? I know it cannot be.
Our ships shall sail upon another sea;
New islands yet shall break upon our sight,
New continents of love and truth and might.

                        JOHN W. CHADWICK

Song at Sunrise

Say not that death is king, that night is lord,
That loveliness is passing, beauty dies;
Nor tell me hope's a vain, deceptive dream
Fate lends to life, a pleasing, luring gleam
To light awhile the earth's despondent skies,
Till death brings swift and sure its dread reward.
Say not that youth deceives, but age is true,
That roses quickly pass, while cypress bides,
That happiness is foolish, grief is wise,
That stubborn dust shall choke our human cries.
Death tells new worlds, and life immortal hides
Beyond the veil, which shall all wrongs undo.
This was the tale God breathed to me at dawn
When flooding sunrise told that night was gone.

THOMAS CURTIS CLARK

The Unbelievable

Impossible, you say, that man survives
The grave—that there are other lives?
More strange, O friend, that we should ever rise
Out of the dark to walk below these skies.
Once having risen into life and light,
We need not wonder at our deathless flight.

Life is the unbelievable; but now
That this Incredible has taught us how,
We can believe the all-imagining Power
That breathed the Cosmos forth as a golden flower
Had potence in his breath
To plan us new surprises beyond death—
New spaces and new goals
For the adventure of ascending souls.

Be brave, O heart, be brave:
It is not strange that man survives the grave:
'Twould be a stranger thing were he destroyed
Than that he ever vaulted from the void.

EDWIN MARKHAM

At End

At end of Love, at end of Life,
At end of Hope, at end of Strife,
At end of all we cling to so,
The sun is setting, must we go?

At dawn of Love, at dawn of Life,
At dawn of Peace, that follows Strife,
At dawn of all we long for so—
The sun is rising, let us go!

LOUISE CHANDLER MOULTON

Some Day or Other

Some day or other I shall surely come
  Where true hearts wait for me;
Then let me learn the language of that home
  While here on earth I be,
Lest my poor lips for want of words be dumb
  In that High Company.

LOUISE CHANDLER MOULTON

The Sea of Faith (From *Passage to India*)

Passage, immediate passage! The blood burns in my veins!
Away, O soul! Hoist instantly the anchor!
Cut the hawsers—haul out—shake out every sail!
Have we not stood here like trees in the ground long
    enough?
Have we not groveled here long enough, eating and
    drinking like mere brutes?
Have we not darkened and dazed ourselves with books
    long enough?

Sail forth—steer for the deep water only,
Reckless, O soul, exploring, I with thee and thou with me,
For we are bound whither mariner has not yet dared
    to go,
And we will risk the ship, ourselves and all.

O my brave soul!
O farther, farther sail!
O daring joy, but safe! Are they not all the seas of God?
O farther, farther sail!

                                        WALT WHITMAN

Death Stands Above Me

Death stands above me, whispering low
    I know not what into my ear:
Of his strange language all I know
    Is, there is not a word of fear.

                            WALTER SAVAGE LANDOR

From *In Memoriam*

Be near me when my light is low,
    When the blood creeps, and the nerves prick
    And tingle; and the heart is sick,
And all the wheels of Being slow.

Be near me when the sensuous frame
    Is racked with pangs that conquer trust;
    And Time, a maniac scattering dust,
And Life, a Fury slinging flame.

Be near me when my faith is dry,
   And men the flies of latter spring,
   That lay their eggs, and sting and sing
And weave their petty cells and die.

Be near me when I fade away,
   To point the term of human strife,
   And on the low dark verge of life
The twilight of eternal day.

ALFRED TENNYSON

Horizon

I watched a sail until it dropped from sight
Over the rounding sea. A gleam of white,
A last far-flashed farewell, and, like a thought
Slipt out of mind, it vanished and was lost.

Yet to the helmsman standing at the wheel
Broad seas still stretched beneath the gliding keel.
Disaster? Change? He felt no slightest sign,
Nor dreamed he of that far horizon line.

So may it be, perchance, when down the tide
Our dear ones vanish. Peacefully they glide
On level seas, nor mark the unknown bound;
We call it death—to them 'tis life beyond.

ANONYMOUS

Vespers

I know the night is near at hand:
  The mists lie low on hill and bay,
The autumn sheaves are dewless, dry;
  But I have had the day.

Yes, I have had, dear Lord, the day;
  When at thy call I have the night,
Brief be the twilight as I pass
  From light to dark, from dark to light.

S. WEIR MITCHELL

The Inn by the Road

Ne'er was the sky so deep a hue
But that the sun came breaking through;
There never was a night so dark
But wakened to the singing lark;
Nor was there ever a lane so long
It had no turn for the weary throng;
Nor heart so sad that sometime after
There came no sound of lilting laughter:
And Death's not the end—'neath the cold
    black sod—
'Tis the Inn by the Road on our way to God.

C. E. WARNER

The Sea

Far, far away—how far I cannot tell—
There is a Sea which has no bounding shore;
Though men have sought to grasp its mystic lore,
Their search is vain—it keeps its secret well.
Years come and go, and still it wields its spell.
But who shall say that time will evermore
Rebuff our quest? Through some now closèd door,
Which faces east, shall men behold the swell
Of fair blue seas, and they shall surely know
That all its waters are of God, who hides
His brightest goals. Someday, at sunset glow,
They too will venture forth on mighty tides;
And they will see, afar, men come and go,
Inviting them to Life, where light abides.

THOMAS CURTIS CLARK

From *Compensation*

And after he has come to hide
Our lambs upon the other side,
We know our Shepherd and our Guide.

And thus by ways not understood,
Out of each dark vicissitude,
God brings us compensating good.

For Faith is perfected by fears,
And souls renew their youth with years,
And Love looks into heaven through tears.

PHOEBE CARY

Immortality

It must be so, Plato, thou reasonest well!—
Else whence this pleasing hope, this fond desire,
This longing after immortality?
Or whence this secret dread, and inward horror
Of falling into naught? Why shrinks the soul
Back on herself, and startles at destruction?
'Tis the divinity that stirs within us,
'Tis heaven itself that points out an hereafter,
And intimates eternity to man.

JOSEPH ADDISON

The Choice

Think thou and act; tomorrow thou shalt die.
Outstretched in the sun's warmth upon the shore,
Thou say'st: "Man's measured path is all gone o'er;
Up all his years, steeply, with strain and sigh,
Man clomb until he touched the truth; and I
Even I, and he whom it was destined for."

How should this be? Art thou then so much more
Than they who sowed, that thou shouldst reap thereby?

Nay, come up hither. From this wave-washed mound
Unto the furthest flood-brim look with me;
Then reach on with thy thought till it be drowned.
Miles and miles distant though the last line be,
And though thy soul sail leagues and leagues beyond—
Still, leagues beyond those leagues, there is more sea.

DANTE GABRIEL ROSSETTI

The Final Quest

I shall go forth some day
Forgetting the foolishness of song and rhyming,
And slowly travel life's road until twilight
Whispers: "This is the end of earth's journey;
Your pathway
Is now up, past the stars;
Keep on climbing!"
With quick intake of breath,
Eyes wide with wonder at the white gleaming
Chalice of exquisite revelation. . . .
I shall drink, and drinking know the renascence
From death,
And be done with all doubt,
And all dreaming

JOHN RICHARD MORELAND

At Evening Time

I know not what the long years hold
  Of winter days and summer clime;
But this I know: when life grows old,
  It shall be light—at evening time.

I cannot tell what boon awaits
  To greet me with the falling night;
But this I know: beyond the gates,
  At evening time, it shall be light.

THOMAS CURTIS CLARK

The Victors

They have triumphed who have died;
They have passed the porches wide,
Leading from the House of Night
To the splendid lawns of light.
They have gone on that far road
Leading to their new abode,
And from curtained casements we
Watch their going wistfully.

They have won, for they have read
The bright secrets of the dead;
And they gain the deep unknown,
Hearing Life's strange undertone.

In the race across the days
They are victors; theirs the praise,
Theirs the glory and the pride—
They have triumphed, having died!

CHARLES HANSON TOWNE

Requiem

Under the wide and starry sky
Dig the grave and let me lie:
Glad did I live and gladly die,
　　And I laid me down with a will.

This be the verse you grave for me:
Here he lies where he longed to be;
Home is the sailor, home from the sea,
　　And the hunter home from the hill.

ROBERT LOUIS STEVENSON

My Sun Sets to Rise Again

Have you found your life distasteful?
　　My life did, and does, smack sweet.
Was your youth of pleasure wasteful?
　　Mine I saved, and hold complete.
Do your joys with age diminish?
　　When mine fail me, I'll complain.

Must in death your daylight vanish?
My sun sets to rise again.

ROBERT BROWNING

Knowledge

They list for me the things I cannot know:
When came the world? What Hand flung out the light
Of yonder stars? How could a God of right
Ordain for earth an endless tide of woe?
Their word is true; I would not scorn their doubt
Who press their questions of the how and why.
But this I know: that from the star-strewn sky
There comes to me a peace that puts to rout
All brooding thoughts of dread, abiding death;
And too I know, with every fragrant dawn,
That Life is Lord; that, with the Winter gone,
There cometh Spring, a great reviving Breath.
It is enough that life means this to me;
What death shall mean, some sunny Morn shall see.

THOMAS CURTIS CLARK

The Last Invocation

At the last, tenderly,
From the walls of the powerful fortressed house,
From the clasp of the knitted locks—from the
    keep of the well-closed doors,

Let me be wafted.
Let me glide noiselessly forth;
With the key of softness unlock the locks—with
   a whisper
Set ope the doors, O soul!
Tenderly—be not impatient,
(Strong is your hold, O mortal flesh!
Strong is your hold, O love.)

WALT WHITMAN

Death

I am the key that parts the gates of Fame;
I am the cloak that covers cowering Shame;
I am the final goal of every race;
I am the storm-tossed spirit's resting place.

The messenger of sure and swift relief,
Welcomed with wailings and reproachful grief,
The friend of those that have no friend but me,
I break all chains, and set all captives free.

I am the cloud that when earth's day is done,
An instant veils an unextinguished sun;
I am the brooding hush that follows strife,
The waking from a dream that man calls—life.

FLORENCE EARLE COATES

From *Snowbound*

Yet Love will dream and Faith will trust,
Since He who knows our need is just,
That somewhere, somehow, meet we must.
Alas for him who never sees
The stars shine through his cypress trees!
Who, hopeless, lays his dead away,
Nor looks to see the breaking day
Across the mournful marbles play!
Who hath not learned, in hours of faith,
The truth to flesh and sense unknown,
That Life is ever Lord of Death,
And Love can never lose its own!

JOHN GREENLEAF WHITTIER

The Last Adventure

All forms of life are endless; each frail vase
   Is emptied o'er and o'er—but filled again;
And never tangled is the wondrous maze
Of nature's melodies through the endless days—
   And yet forever new and sweet to men.

Gleams hint that life upon some future waits;
   The worm cannot forecast the butterfly—
And yet the transformation but creates
A step in the same nature which now mates
   Our own—and may life's mystery untie.

Mayhap the butterfly this message brings:
  "The law, uncomprehended, I obey;
Although the lowliest of earth-bred things,
Even I have been reborn with urgent wings,
  And heavenward fly—who crept but yesterday."

In life's fair mansion I am but a guest;
  And life will bring fulfillment of the gleam.
I trust this last adventure is the best,
The crowning of this earthly life's behest,
  The consummation of the poet's dream.

                                    JAMES TERRY WHITE

The Journey

When Death, the angel of our higher dreams,
Shall come, far ranging from the hills of light,
He will not catch me unaware; for I
Shall be as now communing with the dawn.
For I shall make all haste to follow him
Along the valley, up the misty slope
Where life lets go and Life at last is born.
There I shall find the dreams that I have lost
On toilsome earth, and they will guide me on,
Beyond the mists unto the farthest height.
I shall not grieve except to pity those
Who cannot hear the songs that I shall hear!

                                    THOMAS CURTIS CLARK

Fear Not Thou!

I vex me not with brooding on the years
That were ere I drew breath: why should I then
Distrust the darkness that may fall again
When life is done? Perchance in other spheres—
Dead planets—I once tasted mortal tears,
And walked as now amid a throng of men,
Pondering things that lay beyond my ken,
Questioning death, and solacing my fears.
Ofttimes indeed strange sense have I of this,
Vague memories that hold me with a spell,
Touches of unseen lips upon my brow,
Breathing some incommunicable bliss!
In years foregone, O Soul, was all not well?
Still lovelier life awaits thee. Fear not thou!"

THOMAS BAILEY ALDRICH

No Star Is Ever Lost

No star is ever lost we once have seen,
We may be always what we might have been.
Since Good, though only thought, has life and breath—
God's life—can always be redeemed from death;
And evil, in its nature, is decay,
And any hour can blot it all away;
The hopes that lost in some far distance seem
May be the truer life, and this the dream.

ADELAIDE ANNE PROCTER

The Ways of Death

The ways of Death are soothing and serene,
   And all the words of Death are grave and sweet,
   From camp and church, the fireside and the street,
She signs to come, and strife and song have been.

The summer night descending cool and green
   And dark, on daytime's dust and stress and heat,
The ways of Death are soothing and serene,
   And all the words of Death are grave and sweet.

O glad and sorrowful, with triumphant mien
   And hopeful faces look upon and greet
   This last of all, your lover's, and to meet
Her kiss, the Comforter's, your spirit lean—
The ways of Death are soothing and serene.

                   WILLIAM ERNEST HENLEY

Traveler

Death will ride with me as a friend
Someday, when I cannot see
The curve of the road and the slant of a hill;
When no longer I feel the wind
On my face and the pain of the cold,
A firm hand will be placed on the wheel.

And I'll travel at ease to my journey's end
As one who rides by the side of a friend.

REBEKAH CROUSE COSTANZO

Assurance

If life has naught for us beyond this earth—
A few brief, zestful years, then rayless night;
If that which buoys our hearts, that inner light,
Is but a hope which in our fears has birth;
If only these we have: bright childhood dreams,
Youth's forward urge, strong manhood's valiant deeds,
Then sweet old age, which loving memory feeds—
These are enough, though false all future gleams.
To view one dawn is worth a lifetime's price;
To greet one spring, that will long griefs repay;
To trust one friend makes glad a pilgrim way:
Though night come fast, these will our hearts suffice.
They will suffice—and yet, beyond the night,
There waits a day of days, an undreamed light!

THOMAS CURTIS CLARK

In My Father's House

No, not cold beneath the grasses,
    Not close-walled within the tomb;
Rather, in our Father's mansion,
    Living, in another room.

Living, like the man who loves me,
   Like my child with cheeks abloom,
Out of sight, at desk or schoolbook,
   Busy, in another room.

Nearer than my son whom fortune
   Beckons where the strange lands loom;
Just behind the hanging curtain,
   Serving, in another room.

Shall I doubt my Father's mercy?
   Shall I think of death as doom,
Or the stepping o'er the threshold
   To a bigger, brighter room?

Shall I blame my Father's wisdom?
   Shall I sit enswathed in gloom,
When I know my loves are happy,
   Waiting in another room?

                              ROBERT FREEMAN

Alabaster

From rough stone we are carved.
Chisels dig into the flesh
And hammers beat the bones.
Let old winds blow
The powdered stone away.

Then the white soul shall stand,
An alabaster god
Against a purple sky—
Chiselings at its feet,
And maul and hammer on the floor,
Because the Great Hand is through.

Senility will veil
This god with silver gossamer;
Eternity will unveil it.

RAYMOND KRESENSKY

Good Night

Good night! Good night!
Far from us day takes its flight,
But ever God's eternal love
Remains to guard us, as above
The stars watch with celestial light.
 Good night! Good night!

Till tomorrow! Till tomorrow!
Ah, we know not what may follow.
Close our eyes tonight we may,
Shall we see another day?
Mayhap in vain we say tomorrow,
 Till tomorrow!

VICTOR HUGO

Emigravit

With sails full set, the ship her anchor weighs.
Strange names shine out beneath her figurehead.
What glad farewells with eager eyes are said!
What cheer for him who goes, and him who stays!
Fair skies, rich lands, new homes, and untried days
Some go to seek; the rest but wait instead,
Watching the way wherein their comrades led,
Until the next staunch ship her flag doth raise.
Who knows what myriad colonies there are
Of fairest fields, and rich, undreamed-of gains
Thick-planted in the distant shining plains
Which we call sky because they lie so far?
Oh, write of me, not "Died in bitter pains,"
But "Emigrated to another star!"

HELEN HUNT JACKSON

And So at Last

And so at last, it may be you and I
In some far realm of blue Infinity
Shall find together some enchanted shore
Where Life and Death and Time shall be no more,
Leaving Love only and Eternity.
When each concession Time from Life has wrung,
Like outworn garments from the Soul be flung,
And it shall stand erect, no longer bent,

Slave to the lash of Life's environment,
Even this great world of ours may shrink at last
To some bare Isla Blanca of the past—
A rock unnoticed in the mighty sea
Whose solemn pulse beat marks Eternity.

DAVID STARR JORDAN

Crossing the Bar

Sunset and evening star,
    And one clear call for me!
And may there be no moaning of the bar,
    When I put out to sea.

But such a tide as moving seems asleep,
    Too full for sound and foam,
When that which drew from out the boundless deep
    Turns again home.

Twilight and evening bell,
    And after that the dark!
And may there be no sadness of farewell,
    When I embark;

For though from out our bourne of Time and Place
    The flood may bear me far,
I hope to see my Pilot face to face
    When I have crossed the bar.

ALFRED TENNYSON

AUTHORS' INDEX